THE
LANGUAGE
OF
THIEVES

———

THE LANGUAGE
of
THIEVES

*My Family's Obsession
with a Secret Code
the Nazis Tried to Eliminate*

Martin Puchner

W. W. NORTON & COMPANY
Independent Publishers Since 1923

For information about permission to reproduce selections from this book, write to
Permissions, W. W. Norton & Company, Inc., 500 Fifth Avenue, New York, NY 10110

For information about special discounts for bulk purchases, please contact
W. W. Norton Special Sales at specialsales@wwnorton.com or 800-233-4830

Manufacturing by Sheridan
Book design by Anna Knighton
Production manager: Anna Oler

Library of Congress Cataloging-in-Publication Data

Names: Puchner, Martin, 1969– author.
Title: The language of thieves : my family's obsession with a secret code
the Nazis tried to eliminate / Martin Puchner.
Description: First edition. | New York : W. W. Norton & Company, 2020. |
Includes bibliographical references and index.
Identifiers: LCCN 2020015918 | ISBN 9781324005919 (hardcover) |
ISBN 9781324005926 (epub)
Subjects: LCSH: German language—Slang. | Cant—Germany. | Thieves—
Language. | Tramps—Language. | Language policy—Germany—History—20th
century. | Germany—Languages—Political aspects. | Puchner, Martin, 1969– |
Puchner, Martin, 1969- —Family. | College teachers—United States—Biography.
Classification: LCC PF5995 .P835 2020 | DDC 437.009—dc23
LC record available at https://lccn.loc.gov/2020015918

W. W. Norton & Company, Inc., 500 Fifth Avenue, New York, N.Y. 10110
www.wwnorton.com

W. W. Norton & Company Ltd., 15 Carlisle Street, London W1D 3BS

1 2 3 4 5 6 7 8 9 0

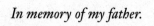

In memory of my father.

Contents

THE
LANGUAGE
OF
THIEVES

———

LANGUAGE GAMES

———

They appeared out of nowhere. Strange figures, dressed in long coats that had lost their original colors, bags slung across their backs. When it rained, they smelled, and my mother wouldn't let them inside the house. "I know what you want. Wait. I'll be right back." I hid behind her for protection. Lingering near the door, I would hear noises from the kitchen, my mother fixing open-faced sandwiches. Plenty of butter and cold cuts, she knew how they liked it. She would return carrying a plate and a glass of water: "Here." While they ate, she remained standing on the threshold, guarding the house, trying to make conversation. The men mostly stared at the food as they ate, avoiding her eye. I had trouble understanding them because they spoke a strange dialect, mixed with words I didn't know. When they had finished, my mother would take the empty plate from their hands and close the door, relieved that the encounter was over. I would run to the window to catch a final glimpse of these men as they disappeared around the corner.

"Who are they?"

"They don't have a home. We're giving them something to eat."

Not very helpful; that much I had observed. I wanted to know why: why didn't they have a home; why were we giving them something to eat; and why did they have such a strange way of talking?

It was the early seventies, I was a few years old, and we were renting a small row house in Nuremberg, Germany, in a quiet part of town. Most of the modest houses had been built in the 1950s because Nuremberg was carpet-bombed during the war and rebuilt cheaply and haphazardly afterward. Despite its towering castle and medieval center, Nuremberg was a manufacturing town with a large working class, supplemented by an influx of foreign workers from Italy, Greece, and Turkey. Some lived on the other side of a park near us, and after I was beaten up by a small group of somewhat older boys—not too badly, really—my mother told me to stay away from them and not stray too far from our own, safer, part of town.

How did those mysterious men find their way to our house, as if guided by a secret hand? Later, my father taught me some of their words. A barn was a *stinker*, prison was *schul* (school), and the entire language was called Rotwelsch. *Welsch*: had these men come all the way from Wales? *Rot*, in German, meant red. Red-Welsh? The whole thing sounded as if a demon had gotten hold of words and played around with them, twisting their meanings for sheer fun. I asked my father, sensing that he might tell me more about these men and their language. "They are travelers," he said. I didn't understand. "Where are they going?" "They are people of the road, escaping to nowhere." It was a strange expression I didn't grasp, but it stayed with me.

My uncle figured out why these escape artists kept showing up at our house when he found a sign discreetly carved into the foundation stone, a cross with a circle around it. He explained that it meant that there was bread to be had here (only they didn't call it bread; they called it *lechem*). There were dozens of such signs. A hammer meant that you had to work in exchange for food; a cat, that an old woman was living on her own. Vertical bars warned of aggressive policemen who would put you in "school."

I was delighted. I couldn't read or write yet, to my shame, and wouldn't learn to until I was almost nine years old, because of dyslexia. My *E*s pointed backward, my *L*s were upside down, individual letters kept getting mixed up; when I tried to read, my eyes darted back and forth, trying to line up words in the right order. It was hopeless. But now my uncle was showing me different types of signs that I could decipher with ease. Sensing my interest, he would draw these signs on pieces of paper, teaching me a good dozen of them.

I learned that travelers left these signs for one another out of solidarity, telling others where to beg, which houses to approach, and which to avoid. They were making the road navigable for their ilk. There were other signs, more complicated, signatures of travelers who wished to make their presence known and who told little stories about what they were up to.[1]

For me, these signs pointed to an underground of traveling people, hidden away from view. In addition to our world, the world of houses and kindergartens (and alphabets), there was a second world inhabited by people of the road, without houses or kindergartens, and with a completely different way of speaking and writing.

The signs were called *zinken*, a word derived from the Latin *signum*, and they turned the world, my world, into a labyrinth of mysterious symbols—and also into a puzzle I wanted to solve, a giant treasure hunt. Finding them became an obsession.

I don't know whether my mother erased the *zinken* directing travelers to our house, but we soon moved away, leaving the travelers behind. On our new street, I saw a traveler only once, an itinerant knife grinder. I ran to the kitchen to take some knives to be sharpened. Timidly, I approached, handed over the knives, and tried out a few Rotwelsch words. The knife grinder looked nonplussed and mumbled something vague. "He didn't understand me," I complained afterward. "He was probably a Gypsy," my mother said. "They use a different language and stick to themselves." She was angry about the price he had charged, while I was mulling over the fact that the road was becoming complicated: there were different groups, different signs, different languages, and the more I learned, the more confusing it became. My uncle once showed me a *zinken* left behind by a traveler who announced, for those who could read it, that he spoke four languages. Another vagrant used a parrot *zinken* to boast of his linguistic prowess.[2]

Later, when I began to study languages, it seemed to me that these signs were the beginning of writing, that they were the product of the basic desire we all share for making marks in the world, for leaving tracks that those in the know could follow. For the time being, my Rotwelsch wasn't good enough for speaking to the knife grinder, but it was good enough to impress my friends. I would run up to them and claim that they were speaking Rotwelsch without knowing it. This was another thing I had learned from my uncle, that Rotwelsch had rubbed off on German. His favorite example was "being in a pickle." As an idiom, it didn't make sense. A pickle was a delicious snack, so why should it have anything to do with being in trouble? Because there was a Rotwelsch expression for "having a difficult time," that sounded, in German, like "being in a pickle" and was therefore assimilated into German (and later, into English).[3] Yes, dear reader: you, too, have been speaking Rotwelsch without knowing it.

I played the "You speak Rotwelsch" trick with everyone I knew, thrilled that I had access to a secret source of information. My own favorite Rotwelsch expression was *an hasn machn*, "making a rabbit," which described not some kind of rabbit stew, but the act of making a quick escape. The phrase captured the earthy wit of this language and its speakers, for whom being in a pickle often meant that they needed to make a rabbit in order to avoid the police. That was another reason that I loved Rotwelsch: it sounded worldly-wise, slightly cynical, suspicious of grand ideas and false words. In Rotwelsch, you knew that life was hard, that survival hinged on reading a faded sign, on making a quick getaway. The language captured an entire mode of life.

I knew that we weren't part of the itinerant underground. We were a perfectly ordinary middle-class family, my mother a primary school teacher, my father an architect. But somehow, through Rotwelsch, I grew up feeling that I had a special

A vagrant identified by the sign MA passed by here on December 22, 1832, with two men (the two vertical lines) and three women or children (three zeros), taking the direction indicated by the arrow.

connection to the road and the itinerant underground, which no one else, none of my friends or my parents' friends, knew anything about. They didn't notice the secret signs on the side of the road or on solitary farms, nor did they know any Rotwelsch expressions—except for the ones they used unwittingly. For me, Rotwelsch became our special possession, our secret. All families develop a special language, words and references no outsider can understand. My family's special language was Rotwelsch.

═══

The main source of all knowledge about Rotwelsch was my father's brother, Uncle Günter. He lived in a sprawling prewar apartment in the bohemian part of Munich, with a swing in the middle of the main corridor. The apartment still bore traces of its earlier incarnation, when my uncle and my father lived there through most of the sixties in a kind of commune. People drifted in and out; it was never quite clear who actually lived there and who was just crashing for a night or a month. It was an unruly place populated with writers, graphic designers, and professional drunks, dressed in bell-bottom corduroy pants, beards, mustaches, and lumberjack shirts.

By the time I was born, the apartment was inhabited only by Günter, my aunt Heidi, and my three cousins. My favorite place in the apartment, besides the swing, was my uncle's study, which had all kinds of instruments—lutes, violas, old violins—hanging on the wall and floor-to-ceiling bookcases full of strange reference books and pamphlets. The pièce de résistance was a contraption he had invented that allowed him to read while lying on his back with books placed on top of a

A peddler of pictures who speaks
four languages. (The triangular
cones mean "being at home"
in four different countries.)

A thief known for speaking
many languages (parrot).

glass frame above his head. I can still see him, with his flowing red beard, reclining on his couch to demonstrate his invention. There was always a smell of sweet smoke, perhaps a result of the hookah up on a bookshelf, mixed in with lingering smoke of pipes and cigarillos, which my father favored.

The study was the place where dictionaries of strange words and obscure treatises on language could be found, old tomes that looked forbidding and intriguing at the same time. It was the source of my uncle's knowledge of Rotwelsch, a mysterious place from which emanated everything that was special about our family and its strange connection to travelers making their way across the face of the earth, going nowhere in particular.

＝

When I was twelve years old, my uncle died of a brain aneurysm. I pictured him lying on his custom-built reading couch, a book of Rotwelsch suspended above his face. He was in his forties, his death was completely unexpected, and the family was in disarray. I overheard snippets of conversation suggesting that he had not died in his study, as I had imagined, but had moved out and was living somewhere else. There were problems with money and inheritance. No one explained anything to me or my younger brother. We were a family that talked a lot, a convivial family. My parents threw lots of parties and arranged chamber concerts at home. There were always people visiting, and I could have as many friends over as I wanted. But about unpleasant things, we did not speak; instead, we played games with Rotwelsch.

After my uncle died, no one wanted to play Rotwelsch anymore. Perhaps it was a painful subject, associated primarily with him, his life choices, and the chaos surrounding his death. I was, reluctantly, entering puberty and had other things on my mind. And so, this language, once a source of mystery and fun, drifted into the background, an eccentric hobby that had captivated us for a time.

But somehow, Rotwelsch stayed with me, and when I look back now, I realize that it shaped my life more than I knew at the time. It attuned me to the underground of words, to the byways of language. As I learned more about Rotwelsch, I found the language ensconced in a battle over migration and national identity that had lasted since the Middle Ages. After I immigrated to the United States, I learned that Rotwelsch, and the battles surrounding it, had followed me to the New World.

But the biggest mystery was why my own family was so strangely entangled with this secret language. It turned out that not only my uncle and father but also my grandfather had been obsessed with it. The process of researching this history brought me face-to-face with family secrets and evasions, with historical guilt and attempts at atonement.

Chapter 1

CAMOUFLAGE NAMES

———

Twenty years after my induction into Rotwelsch, I was sitting in Harvard's Widener Library, beginning my graduate studies in comparative literature. Widener seemed the best place in the world for studying languages because it housed pretty much every book ever written. "Housed" is not quite the right word. One of the things I've learned is to pay attention to words, to call things by their proper names. In the case of Widener, the building doesn't house the books so much as the books, all six million of them, hold up the building. The shelves run from floor to ceiling and are both weight and weight-bearing wall at the same time: they are what keeps the entire building from collapsing.

I was surprised, but thrilled, to have ended up here. In school, I had studied as many languages as I could, learning French, Latin, and English. In college, I had added Greek and then went to study in Italy, picking up some Italian in the process.

It wasn't so much that I was particularly good at languages—I was okay—but that learning languages exerted a strange fascination on me. New languages allowed me entry into new worlds that had been inaccessible to me, and I was only dimly aware that this interest resonated with the enigmatic figures who had shown up at our house with their *zinken* and secret words. Subliminally, Rotwelsch had taught me a lesson: we speak not only to reveal our thoughts but also to hide them; we create community with shared codes, but also by making sure that no outsider can understand them.

It was getting late, I couldn't concentrate on what I was reading, and I found myself thinking instead about the library and its vast holdings. That's when the idea hit me to look up my grandfather. He had been a librarian and a historian, specializing in the history of names. He was also interested in family history and, in his spare time, had traced ours back centuries to a farm called the Puchhof in southern Germany. This was his usual method, to relate names to specific locations. He had spent his life connecting words to the landscape, tracking the way in which humans had made the earth their own by naming it. It was a specialty that I had always found slightly comical yet strangely compelling.

I mostly remember him in retirement, sitting in his armchair with a pipe in his mouth; sometimes he would order my grandmother around with his cane, but more as a joke; it was really she who called the shots by then. We often made fun of him and he was mostly good-humored about it. His cane and the bad leg came from the war, a wound that hurt whenever the barometer was falling. I imagined that a piece of shrapnel was still stuck in his leg, a piece of the war, like a message from the past, that was lodged inside of him and couldn't be removed.

My grandparents lived on the outskirts of Munich in a house surrounded by a garden full of plum trees. In the fall, we would harvest the plums, and my grandmother would bake them into cinnamon-scented pies, while the remaining plums would fall to the ground and rot, drawing droves of wasps. These harvests were family affairs and included several cousins as well as my aunt Roswitha, my father's younger sister. My grandfather would be sitting on the terrace, watching the jolly spectacle with satisfaction.

Would Widener have any of his works? I checked out the card catalogue, a room with drawers full of index cards (which would shortly be replaced with computers). Puchner. Karl Puchner. There was his name, close to where mine might be found, one day. I was sent to the basement floor and from there through a tunnel to an underground library, from which an elevator took me down even farther to a small library dug deep into the ground, called Pusey 3. It was empty and silent, the place where librarians had safely tucked away old church history and other subjects better not exposed to the light of day.

It was here that I found my grandfather's dissertation, from 1932, about patron saints of monasteries in a diocese in southern Germany.[1] The dissertation was essentially a list of monasteries, one after the other, with a thumbnail sketch of when each had adopted its patron saint. I was mildly interested to see that one of the patron saints was Saint Martin. Other publications of his I found were similar, medieval manuscripts, histories of important families and monasteries. I also came across a very short biography, attached to his dissertation, in which he informed his readers, in the first person, that he was born in Nuremberg as the son of a lower-ranking business clerk, graduated from high school, studied to become a teacher of history, geography, and literature, passed the teacher's examination, and had then written his dissertation.

Even compared with the obscure literature I tended to study, his writings were hard going, and I was slightly disappointed. What had I hoped to find? Probably something that would tell me more about him, something expressing a little personality. But perhaps this was his personality: doing historical drudge work, preserving documents that would enable future historians to reconstruct the past.

I looked around for what else I might find and finally located a scholarly journal with an article by him. Leafing through it casually, I chanced upon an unexpected word: Rotwelsch. I hadn't known that my grandfather had been interested in this language as well. Was this how his sons, my father and my uncle, had first learned about it?

I examined the article more carefully, including its title: "Family Names as Racial Markers."[2] Puzzled, I started to read, first curiously, then faster and faster, with increasing alarm. My grandfather was worried about the confusions that might be created by names. Some names sounded Jewish, even though the family was Aryan. In other instances, a name sounded perfectly German, but the family that claimed it was Jewish. It was a huge problem. Fortunately, my grandfather also knew a solution, one that fit neatly within his own field of study. He recommended that language experts such as himself should distinguish between Jewish-sounding German names and German-sounding Jewish names. He was volunteering to participate in this effort, which he considered crucial for the future of the German State.

Frantically, my mind went over everything I knew about him. The work on family names and family history, which had seemed benign, took on a different quality when it was connected to race. Wasn't this precisely what the Nazis had done, requiring everyone, the entire nation, to become genealogists, tracing their family back and hoping, or pretending, that there was no drop of Jewish blood? On the back of the journal, I saw advertisements for various products connected to genealogy, including a kit for building your own home registry of names, an introduction to family names, and a book called *Biological Will*. Everyone was required to produce an official genealogical table, called an Ancestor Passport, tracing the family back at least two generations. Names and race: an essential topic in Germany in 1934, the perfect time to start a career as a historian of names.

Shaken, I forced myself to read the article more slowly. It was set in the gothic font preferred by the Nazis, which I wasn't used to. Somewhat haltingly, I realized that the article had been based on a lecture. Despite his hateful tone, he knew a lot about the topic. Clearly my grandfather had been studying Jewish names for years.

Names, I learned from the article, contained within them the entire history of peoples and populations. Place-names, his specialty, carried information about who had moved through a given region by naming it. Now my grandfather found that personal names could tell him about the places people had lived in. It was exactly his usual method of connecting names to places, only in reverse.

For a long time, Jewish names were based on the Bible, but the volatile history of the Near East meant that Jews soon used non-Hebrew names as well. My grandfather singled out Greek names, the result of Alexander the Great and his conquest of the Near East, which had made Greek the lingua franca of the region. Mostly, Jews (and many non-Jews) went by first names, adding "son of X" for convenience. Only the descendants of Levites and the priestly class used hereditary last names such as Levi or Cohn.

Once Jewish migrants arrived in Germany in the early Middle Ages, they began using German names as well. My grandfather listed among them names of places, and noted that those names could be used to track the settlement of Jews in Germany. There were few Jewish names connected to locations in the far north of Germany, a region in which Jews had not been allowed to settle for periods of time. Instead, he noted a high frequency of these names along the Rhine, partially because the river facilitated trade, but also around Nuremberg—although not in Nuremberg itself, because from 1499 to 1806 that city didn't allow Jews to spend even a single night within its walls. Frankfurt, by contrast, was one of the centers of Jewish settlement, as could be told by the fact that many Jews had adopted the name of the city, Frankfurter. They even used names of specific buildings in the city. Since houses weren't numbered, they were named after distinct features, the name Rothschild (which means red sign) being a prominent example. Other names derived from professions, especially those having to do with trade.

The most crucial innovation in Jewish names came in the eighteenth century, when Enlightenment ideas induced rulers to emancipate the Jews by giving them equal rights as citizens and subjects. The movement began with Joseph II, emperor of Austria, who was influenced by Voltaire, the leading Enlightenment philosopher. In order to make Jews full subjects in the eyes of the state, they had to choose hereditary last names, hence the unusual names of Ashkenazi (Yiddish- and German-speaking) Jews, names often based on plants (Rosenzweig, or Rose-Twig), ornaments (Goldblatt, or Gold-Leaf), and other fanciful objects. One by one, other European states followed suit, until even Russia granted Jews equal rights as subjects of the czar in 1845.

My grandfather didn't present this history of Jewish settlement, from biblical times through exile and to emancipation, neutrally. The Enlightenment emancipation, for example, he called the most unfortunate idea of them all, leading to the "Jewification" of German life. Jewification—Hitler's favorite word.³

If my grandfather derided the emancipation of the Jews as the worst mistake in history, there was one thing he found amusing about it, as a historian of names. Joseph II of Austria had made all kinds of rules about the names Jews could adopt. No biblical names were allowed, nor the names of places or those based on professions because there were already too many of those. The new names should be unique, making it easier to identify each individual.

The emperor put his civil servants in charge of overseeing the imposition of appropriate names, and my grandfather noted that while some names were pretty, others, imposed on Jews by low-level functionaries, were deliberately ridiculous and humiliating, such as Mr. Dung (Mist, in German) or Mrs. Sewer-Cover (Kanalgitterbestandteil). In this situation, some Jews managed to bribe functionaries and effectively buy less-humiliating names, but the rest were out of luck. These names captured the particularly cruel sense of humor of those who imposed them. When soldiers were in charge, for example, the names they came up with would be Mr. Gun-Cleaner (Gewehrreiniger) or Mrs. Gunpowder (Schießpulverbestandteil). The wit of soldiers, my grandfather called it, and probably chuckled. I could imagine his audience chuckling as well. He hinted that there were names he did not wish to mention in polite company, probably causing more chuckling and knowing eye-rolling among his audience in March 1934.

Amusing as all this might be, my grandfather conceded, he didn't regard the naming of Jews as a laughing matter. The problem was that Jews had assumed German names in such numbers that one couldn't distinguish a German from a Jew. Before the enforced diversification of Jewish names, Jews had often adopted the names of cities in which they lived, but so had many Germans. Jews had names connected to trade, but so did Germans. Yes, one might find clues by noticing names based on cities with large Jewish communities and deduce Jewish ancestry from that. Frankfurter was almost always a Jewish name, while Nuremberger was almost always German. But there was no real certainty. Even in the case of Old Testament names one couldn't be sure that the bearer was Jewish because many Germans had adopted those names as well—even the names Solomon and Israel, my grandfather noted, could be German. Confusion was everywhere. We have to be careful, my grandfather said over and over again to his audience. We simply can't be too careful with this business of names. Jews had used their notorious capacity for adapting to their environment by assuming the names of their host cultures, while deep down sticking to their own ancient traditions.

It wasn't just a matter of confusion, my grandfather said; it was a matter of outright deception. Jews had deliberately adopted Christian-sounding names to deceive. My grandfather coined the term "camouflage name," or *Tarnname*, to iden-

tify this phenomenon.⁴ "The Jew Karl Marx"—a name derived
from the German first name Max—was an example that came
to my grandfather's mind right away. And so many Marxists,
my grandfather helpfully added, were of course Jews. (I'm sure
Karl Puchner also disliked the fact that Karl Marx bore his own
first name.) But what really riled up my grandfather were cases
in which particularly nice German names were being abused in
this way, to give cover to Jews. He singled out the name Siegfried, which had become a popular Jewish first name at the turn
of the century, for particular outrage.

It was in the course of such reflections that my grandfather
addressed the question of language. Yiddish, he observed, the
Hebrew-inflected version of German spoken by Jewish settlers,
was a strange mixture of Hebrew and German, "and like every
mixture, it is disgusting." But for my grandfather, there was one
language mixture that was even more disgusting than Yiddish:
Rotwelsch.

The shifting names of Jews were often associated with
crime, as can be seen by looking at the police records of the
time. It is well-known that the entire Jewry is closely associated with criminality. The so-called Rotwelsch language
is such a mixture of German, Hebrew, and the language
of Gypsies. Unfortunately, spoken German has absorbed
some words from these muddy waters, of Hebrew origin,
such as *schummeln* [cheating], *Tinef* [excrement], *Kaff* [small
village], *schofel* [dishonest], *Moos*, meaning money, and similar terms. Members of criminal gangs didn't use proper
names, in order to hide from the authorities. One file doc-
umenting the cross-examination of a gang numbering over

two hundred members shows that not one of them had a proper name.[5]

The passage didn't make a lot of sense: there was little logical connection between the sentences, merely insinuation. Gang members adopted new names. Jews had changed their names over the course of their history. Hence Jews were gang members. Well, not really. (Also, not all of these words are of Hebrew origin.)

But what was most shocking to me was that this confused rant contained everything that had intrigued me about Rotwelsch, my fascination with secret names, with language mixtures, even with the fact that Rotwelsch expressions had filtered back into German, so that Germans used Rotwelsch expressions without realizing it. All this wasn't exactly wrong, as far as I knew. It certainly was what my uncle and my father had told me about Rotwelsch. Only now my grandfather was using these features as proof that all Jews were criminals.

For his list of Rotwelsch terms that had infiltrated German, my grandfather cherry-picked terms associated with dishonesty (*schummeln* for cheating and *schofel* for dishonest) and disgust (*Tinef* for excrement). Why not use the words and expressions I loved, such as "making a rabbit" for making an escape, or "school" for prison? Or, if you have to, "stinker" for barn? Rotwelsch was no "muddy water," as my grandfather dismissively called it. It was inventive, funny, touching, and, above all, mysterious.

Also, while I didn't know much about Yiddish, my grandfather's dismissive remarks made it clear that the fates of the two languages, Rotwelsch and Yiddish, were intertwined. They certainly had managed to make similar enemies.

I forced myself to finish the article. At the end, he made several policy recommendations:

1. The creation of a registry of Jewish names. He ominously hinted that practical actions could be based on such a registry with regard to the "Jewish question."
2. To end centuries of deceptive practices, Jews should no longer be allowed to change their names.
3. Jews should be forcibly stripped of German first names.

My head was spinning as a flood of memories, emotions, and questions crashed into one another. A Polaroid photograph I had kept from my childhood shows my grandfather with my brother, me, and one of my brother's innumerable teddy bears. I'm holding a book called *The Makers' Book for Boys*; it promised to teach boys how to make everything from model airplanes to fancy stereo speakers. At first I loved the idea that I could make all those things myself, but over the years the book brought me much unhappiness, since nothing I tried to make from it ever quite worked.

Then there was the time when he had taken me to a restaurant, which was exciting because my family didn't go to restaurants very often. I chose *Schäufele*, a piece of pig's shoulder that was called *shovel* after the shape of the shoulder bone. (I have since become a vegetarian.) And now I found out that my good-humored old grandfather, who was the first to treat me like a grown-up, who bought me pig's shovel, and who had tried to show me how to become a boy who could make things with his own hands, had written this anti-Semitic rant focused on names and language.

My first reaction was deep shame. No one must know about this. As a German living abroad, I had always felt exposed, marked guilty by association, wanting to apologize for crimes committed by my country of birth. And now I found out that it wasn't just a matter of indirect association anymore; it was something deeper, more personal, something lodged within my own family, a matter of genes or some other form of inheritance, something inside of me that I couldn't get rid of and that I would have to keep secret forever.

Then came anger that my grandfather was doing this to me, that he was putting me in this position. Not knowing what to do, I channeled my anger into research. It turned out that my grandfather was no outlier: names were right at the center of Nazi thinking about race. The Nuremberg Laws of 1935 defined as Jewish everyone who had at least three Jewish grandparents. This definition didn't solve the problem—who was Jewish—but only kicked it back two generations. If ancestors self-identified as Jewish through membership in Jewish religious organizations, the case was relatively clear. But what if they didn't, thanks to the emancipation of the Jews that my grandfather deplored so much?

In those cases, Nazi racial science was supposed to decide. But even though the Nazis claimed that their beliefs about race were based on science, they just couldn't make it work. The reason was, and is, that race is not a scientific category. A few negligible, superficial features—skin color; slightly differently shaped facial features—are taken to have profound implications about mental abilities, behavior, and character, which they simply don't. Racial "science" is a complete fabrication; every instance of it has turned out to be pure ideology, the result of prejudice and projection. This is why it could be so successful: people wanted to believe it; they wanted their prejudices, the belief in the superiority of this or that race, confirmed; and they were happy to have those prejudices, from those prevalent in nineteenth-century America to twentieth-century Germany, dressed up as science. Race in that sense, the belief that humans can be divided in meaningful ways according to "races"—that systems of classifying races have anything substantial to say about humans, their abilities and behaviors—is simply without foundation.

The only thing about race that is real is racism. The history of race is really a history of racism and the attempts to grapple with the consequences of racism. This was a huge problem for the Nazis, because it meant that Nazi scientists couldn't distinguish between Jews and Germans by measuring noses, foreheads, or the distance between the ears. As Nazis passed more laws about Jews, their inability to come up with scientific tests that would tell them who was Jewish became an embarrassment.

In the absence of biological criteria, names became crucial, and this was where my grandfather sensed an opportunity. He was waving his flag as a historian of names, promising to deliver what biologists could not. His registry would help sort

Jews from non-Jews, the distinction on which the entire Nazi state was now based. Instead of the "science" of race, he recommended the "science" of names.

Most of my grandfather's recommendations dovetailed with Nazi policies. In 1938, a few years after the Nuremberg Laws were passed, Jews were no longer allowed to change their names. To make things simple, the list of acceptable Jewish names was limited to 185 for men and 91 for women.[6] Most biblical names were forbidden. On January 1, 1939, all Jews still bearing non-official names were automatically renamed: men were registered as Israel and women as Sarah.[7] I doubt that these measures were adopted because of my grandfather's advocacy; he wasn't important enough for that. But his ideas clearly overlapped with official policy, and he must have been pleased to see them become the law of the land.

There was one problem with the registry of Jewish names: bureaucratic infighting. The theory of the state promoted by Nazis was based on a strict hierarchy, a pyramid ascending toward the all-powerful leader. The practice was pretty much the opposite. Hitler kept his inner circle on their toes by playing them off against one another and by keeping them guessing how much power and influence each of them had. Whenever one rose above the others, Hitler would humiliate him (they were all men). None ever knew exactly where he stood.

This ambiguity affected all organs of state, including those charged with creating a registry of Jewish names.[8] There was the Federal Agency of Genealogy (Reichsstelle für Sippenforschung), which produced an alphabetical registry with an estimated 800 million card entries. At the same time, there was the General Archive of German Jews, which contained the membership information of the Association of German Jews.

On a local level, parish registries and communal registries had records on Jewish inhabitants. There was also the police, especially the secret police force created by the Nazis (Gestapo), which started its own registry of Jewish names. Yet another source of information about Jews was the census, which used the Hollerith machine, the latest in information technology from America.[9] A precursor of modern computers, it was originally used to process U.S. census data, beginning in 1888. Its punch cards and dials were now used to process information on Jewish names.

Technology couldn't solve the competition among the different agencies charged with Jewish affairs, which meant that the single registry of Jewish names my grandfather proposed was never created. In the end, the Nazis were forced to rely on Jewish organizations to supply lists of names, as well as on their own patchwork of registries and archives for people they considered Jewish but who were not members of Jewish organizations. Unfortunately, this administrative mess didn't help the victims very much, for what the Nazis lacked in terms of cooperative organization, they made up for in sheer brutality.

===

I was hardly the only German to discover a Nazi past in the family, but this discovery came to me with an unusual mystery: what did Rotwelsch have to do with it? The language mixture, the secret names, the Yiddish and Hebrew influence—this was what had drawn me to studying languages. Only now my grandfather was shouting, triumphantly, See, this is what I have been saying all along. Jews can't be trusted, they are all thieves, they debase German (muddy waters); they take names and words and distort them deliberately for their own nefarious purposes (camouflage names). They use German to hide their true intentions.

My grandfather made me see that, in a strange, twisted way, Rotwelsch was perfect for anti-Semites. It seemed to confirm their most irrational ideas by connecting language, race, and criminality. This was what my grandfather was proposing: if you can't use biology to detect race, names will do. His program of keeping the German language free from mixture was the equivalent of the Nazi dream of keeping German blood from mixing with Jewish blood. From this perspective, Rotwelsch, this language of mixture, was inherently suspect, and, adding insult to injury, it made a mockery of German, much like the Jewish practice of using names like Siegfried. Jews were polluters of language and language thieves.

I realized that even though I had grown up around Rotwelsch, I knew next to nothing about its history. Was it possible that Jews deliberately used Hebrew to create a secret language? Was it true that Rotwelsch was a Jewish language or, as my grandfather would say, a "typically Jewish" language, a language with which to hide your true identity? Who were its speakers? How had the language developed? And why had my grandfather's two sons, my uncle and my father, decided to introduce Rotwelsch into our lives? Why had my uncle devoted the better part of his adult life to this language, a language his father hated with such intensity? Questions upon questions, mysteries, traces: this was what I normally liked, what I studied, what I was good at. I would have to use my skills—poking around archives, following clues, detecting meaning hidden behind words—for a very different purpose: to uncover the secret of Rotwelsch and its relation to my family. My search led me, unexpectedly, to Martin Luther.

ROTWELSCH LESSON: DON'T TRUST ANYONE

Avoid: a dishonest
person.

Act pious to get
something out of
these people.

A single person
lives here.

Schofel = dishonest

Schummeln = to cheat

Mauscheln = to cheat

Verratzen = to rat on someone; to betray

Amerikanisch mischen = to shuffle American-style; to cheat
by only pretending to shuffle a deck of cards

Gannef = a thief

Macker = a thief

Mausen = to steal

Schoren = to steal

Moos = money

Tinef = excrement

THE BOOK OF VAGRANTS

———

It was the year of the Lord 1521, and Luther had recently spoken in Worms, despite opposition from Rome, in front of the kings and potentates of the Holy Roman Empire. At the meeting, he had faced intense pressure to recant his provocative theses on the limited power of the Pope and the failings of the Church, but he had stuck to his positions with his usual recalcitrance. Because Emperor Charles V had promised Luther safe passage home to Wittenberg, his return voyage had been triumphant. He spoke and preached along the way, reveling in the support of ordinary Christians for his fight against corruption and the abuse of power by the Church.

Amid the exhilaration following his triumph, there was also danger. Luther couldn't be sure that Charles would stick to his promises; and in fact the emperor had ordered Luther arrested as soon as he arrived in Wittenberg. For Luther, the trip home was likely his last moment of freedom.

As his carriage was making its way along the winding mountain roads through the Black Forest, masked riders appeared out of nowhere, bringing the carriage to an abrupt stop. Had Charles become impatient and decided to have Luther arrested on his way home? Had Luther's preaching along the way enraged the emperor enough for him to break his word? Luther was forced out of his carriage and made to mount a horse. The riders took him deep into the wooded mountains, he didn't know to what end. His captors didn't identify themselves, which they would have done had they been acting on behalf of the emperor. Why were they wearing masks?

Being abducted on the road was a routine danger in Martin Luther's late Middle Ages, a world of walls and moats, of kings living in impenetrable castles; burghers, in well-defended towns; monks, in secure monasteries; and farmers, huddled together in villages. Connecting these areas of relative safety was the road, traveled by merchants, journeymen, and pilgrims, but also by runaway apprentices, deserters, escaped convicts, beggars, thieves, and rogues. Perhaps Luther had ended up in the hands of a gang composed of vagrants, also known as highwaymen? Were they hoping to deliver him to Charles for a ransom? Or were they ignorant of whom they had captured?

After some travel on horseback, Luther was taken to a castle. His kidnappers then took off their masks and revealed that he was in the custody of their master, Frederick III of Saxony, also known as Frederick the Wise. The elector was sympathetic to Luther and had abducted him for his own safety, to preempt his arrest by Emperor Charles. Frederick was ready to harbor Luther at Wartburg Castle as long as he remained there in disguise. Luther agreed. He shed his friar's garb and was given knight's clothing, complete with a rapier. He was told to let his beard grow out, as was customary among knights. And he was given a new name: Junker Jörg (Knight George).[1]

Junker Jörg spent the next six weeks furiously translating the New Testament from the original Greek into German, making this source text of Christianity available to the common people. Soon, the result would be published in cheap editions, thanks to the printing press, which had been invented just eighty years earlier.

Initially, Luther had launched his protest against the Catholic Church in a handwritten letter addressed to his bishop in Latin. But Luther's friends recognized that the printing press could become Luther's secret weapon in his seemingly hopeless battle against the Church. After some trial and error, Luther developed a knack for channeling outrage, for articulating the needs of common people. After he left the protective custody of Wartburg Castle, he took his revolt to the streets and into people's homes. Luther thus became the first modern populist.[2]

═══

Luther not only created a new branch of Christianity but also shaped political history. Above all, he deliberately shaped language, modern German, through his translation of the Bible. This was why he took an interest in a strange book called *Liber Vagatorum*, The Book of Vagrants.[3] Originally, it had been written and published anonymously. But now, with his newfound notoriety, Luther was republishing it, with a new preface of his own, so that it might reach a broader public.

The book provided a kind of inventory of different kinds of beggars and vagrants, most of them dishonest. They included deceivers pretending to be escaped prisoners who had been held in northern Africa, fake cripples lingering in front of churches, charlatans offering to exorcise the devil, tramps pretending to be suffering from the falling sickness, ordinary vagrants claiming to be on a pilgrimage, beggars faking blindness or attracting alms by going naked, destitute women claiming to be mad, to have given birth to monsters, to be repentant former prostitutes, or to be suffering from leprosy, as well as men claiming to be former hangmen who were now doing penance. Other vagabonds assumed the air of aristocrats who had fallen on hard times, while yet another group carried Roman tokens to suggest that they had completed a pilgrimage to the Holy City and now needed some funds for their journey home.

These varieties of vagrants weren't violent, but they were dangerous nonetheless because their lies were of the devil and needed to be stopped. Luther was publishing the *Liber Vagatorum* to help his fellow burghers guard against these fraudulent beggars. For Luther, the matter was personal. In his preface, he complained that he himself had been a frequent victim of these "tramps and tongue twisters," adding urgency to his campaign against their treachery. Thieving beggars employed every trick in the book, Luther said, from false garments and false stories to false names, and they needed to be stopped (conveniently, he forgot that he himself had assumed a false name and false garments at Wartburg Castle).

The worst deception, and the most dangerous one, was the way they twisted their words. Luther, who had studied Hebrew, Greek, and Latin, was highly sensitive to language. The *Liber Vagatorum* included a list of 225 words that Luther called Rotwelsch. He was one of the first to name this mysterious language. Not "Red from Wales," as I'd thought. *Rot* was a word for beggar; *welsch* could mean Italian, but mostly it meant incomprehensible. *Rot-welsch*: the incomprehensible cant of beggars.

Luther not only knew the name Rotwelsch; he also recognized that many of the words used by these traveling beggars were derived from Hebrew, a language he had studied in order to read the Old Testament in the original. He concluded: "The Rotwelsch language comes from the Jews."[4]

For Luther, that was not a good thing. In some early tracts, he had spoken highly of Jews as forerunners of Christianity and looked forward to their conversion, but when they refused to listen to him, his enthusiasm waned, and he began to attack them viciously. In his treatise *On the Jews and Their Lies*, he described them as being prone to lying, thieving, and spitting, and denounced them as a vile pestilence and an accursed people.[5] He recommended that their synagogues, schools, and houses be burned to the ground, and that whatever didn't burn should be razed and buried deep enough that nothing remained visible. Luther wanted Jews gone without a trace and hoped that they would be reduced to wandering the earth like Gypsies, chased from place to place for all eternity.

What was the connection between vagrants, Rotwelsch, and Jews? Unlike Luther's preface to the *Liber Vagatorum*, the main text of that book didn't mention Jews, except for a certain Hans von Strasburg, who was described as a quack doctor and a former Jew, presumably converted. Most of the beggars the book lists seem to be Christian. So how come they were speaking a language that "came from the Jews"? Why would the Jews give their language to a random assortment of Christian beggars and vagrants? Luther didn't pause to ask these questions. Rotwelsch, for him, proved that the three groups he disliked most—vagrants, beggars, and Jews—were related.

I tried to disentangle this knot of prejudice and fact. It was clear that Luther disliked Jews, which he rationalized with the old Christian complaint that they were responsible for the death of Jesus, since, according to the Gospels, they had asked their Roman overlord to kill him. Adding insult to injury, Jews had refused to accept Christ into their hearts, stubbornly adhering to their old ways, which included sticking to their sacred text rather than accepting the fact that Jesus had come to fulfill the Hebrew Bible, endowing it with a new spirit. But Luther's hatred of Jews didn't stop at ancient history and theology. In his eyes, they were foreign, migrants who were found wandering across German lands. Luther didn't say anything about the persecutions and expulsions that had forced Jewish communities to be on the move. Nor did he propose to allow them to settle anywhere permanently.

In the same vein, he objected to traveling beggars. Luther conceded that it was permissible to give alms to local, resident beggars, but those from farther away, especially foreign beggars, shouldn't be tolerated; their nefarious tricks needed to be unmasked—with the help of the *Liber Vagatorum*—and then they should be chased away or arrested. God commands us to help the poor, but it is the devil who tempts us into giving alms to vagrants.

Beggars, foreigners, and Jews—they were all mixed together, in Luther's mind, and implicated in his all-consuming fight against Rome and the Catholic Church. The figure of the wandering Jew played a role in associating Jewishness with vagrancy.[6] But Luther was also harsh about mendicants, monks who had sworn an oath of poverty and begged for their sustenance. They might look like devoted Christians, but Luther hated them from the bottom of his heart, because they had deliberately chosen to be poor, living off hardworking people while claiming the support of Rome.

In Luther's mind, the bond holding these distinct groups of people—mendicants, foreign beggars, and Jews—together was Rotwelsch. Because it contained Hebrew words, the language was Jewish in its essence, foreign and hostile to Christendom. And it was a language of vagrants and beggars, of people eternally on the road, escaping to nowhere, as my father had put it.

Luther wasn't worried so much that Jews would convert Christians to Judaism, but he was worried about their words. The Hebrew words Jews had brought to this land were now spreading among the people of the road, worming their way into German, the language that he had just tried to elevate by making it suitable for the holy scripture.

The strange thing was that the *Liber Vagatorum* didn't just warn its readers about Rotwelsch: it was peppered with Rotwelsch words, including the names for different types of beggars and their deceptions. A list of words was attached "so that the words used in the book can be understood." Luther lists *mackum*, for town; *sefel*, for dirt (from Hebrew *shafel* for low to the earth, despicable); *molsamer*, for traitor (*mole* means full, *sam* means poison).

The *Liber Vagatorum* forced its readers to learn Rotwelsch, almost like a foreign-language primer presenting a sample text with a vocabulary list. But why would Luther be giving his readers a taste of this thieves' cant, even though their idiom was foreign, Jewish, and deceptive, the work of the devil? It was almost as if he hoped that the *Liber Vagatorum* would allow readers to experience just how deceptive Rotwelsch was so as to encourage them to reject it.

When I studied Luther's vocabulary list, I noticed two words

in particular: *mess* (or *moos*), for money, and *gfar*, for village
(based on the Hebrew word *kfar*). They were among the words
my grandfather had singled out in his essay against Rotwelsch.
Luther was in the grip of the same illogical combination of
ideas I had also detected in my grandfather, confusing Jews and
vagrants, language, religion, and a mode of life. Clearly, my
grandfather wasn't alone; the roots of his ideas reached deep
into German—Christian—history, with its inchoate beliefs
about race and language all tangled together in a single, messy
knot. Both Luther and my grandfather juxtaposed ideas without explaining how they were connected. Bad logic was an early
warning sign for prejudice.

=

After Luther, and despite his best efforts, Rotwelsch words kept
getting more entangled with the German language as Rotwelsch increased its reach, especially during times of upheaval.
The most terrible upheaval, and therefore the most conducive
to Rotwelsch, was one triggered by Martin Luther himself,
when the Protestant revolution erupted into an all-out religious
war a century after his death. Central Europe was particularly
hard hit because it was the heartland of the Protestant revolution and was fragmented into different kingdoms and duch-
ies, whose rulers kept changing their religious allegiances and
alliances. Gradually, larger powers such as Spain, France, and
Sweden got involved, and mercenary armies financed by these
foreign actors kept invading, looting, living off the land, and
recruiting young men into their armies, often by force, turning German-speaking lands into the battlefield on which a
Europe-wide conflict between Protestants and Catholics was

fought. The war kept getting bigger until it became known as
the Thirty Years War (1618–1648), the longest and most devastating of all religious wars in Europe.[7]

The violence this war unleashed on the civilian population
was unprecedented in its intensity and prompted the French
engraver Jacques Callot to create a series of etchings called *The
Miseries of War*, the first modern antiwar work. The most grue-
some is called *The Hanging* and shows a tree heavy with strange
fruit.

The Thirty Years War was ended with the Peace of Westphalia, which divided a continent hitherto controlled by alliances
among aristocratic families into a checkerboard of nation-
states. Each nation-state was responsible for what was happening within its borders, and promised not to interfere with the
religious predilections of its citizens. The Peace of Westphalia established the modern political order in which we still live
today. Every time we object to regime change, or believe that a
state should not force its citizens to convert to the religion of its
ruler, it is in part because of this treaty.

The new order didn't include everyone. Large numbers of decommissioned soldiers, displaced peasants, and other vagrants continued to ignore the new boundaries. Driven from their native villages and towns, they roamed the countryside, seeking food and shelter, sometimes forming large gangs and associations that could number fifty members or more, taking advantage of the breakdown of civil order.

Rotwelsch was the winner of this postwar chaos. With more speakers and more words, it grew into a full-blown idiom for travelers of all sorts. While it had been a second, "professional" language of itinerant beggars during most of its history, in the aftermath of the Thirty Years War it may well have become something closer to the native tongue of those growing up amid these large roaming gangs.

As Rotwelsch grew, so also grew the opposition to it. Authorities followed Luther's lead and published lists of words and expressions so that upstanding citizens might understand the plotting of itinerant thieves. In order to establish law and order, the secret language of thieves needed to be decoded and exposed, the swamp, or the "muddy waters" my grandfather had written about, drained. There was a language war afoot. The point of this greater war was to keep German pure by expelling vagrants and foreigners from German lands.

My grandfather was a mere foot soldier in this war. This didn't justify what he had written, but it put him in a long tradition. I imagined trying to ask him about Luther, about his hatred of foreign names, foreign people, and vagrants. Did he really believe in the jumbled logic that was poisoning his thought? One thing was clear: Rotwelsch cast a long shadow on German cultural history.

LUTHER'S ROTWELSCH LESSON:
WORDS THAT COME FROM THE JEWS

Acheln = to eat
Betzam = egg
Gfar = village
Lehem = bread
Mackum = town
Molsamer = traitor

MARTIN LUTHER'S
WARNING ABOUT FALSE BEGGARS

Dobissers: These are knaves who pass themselves off for friars and go to peasants to touch them with a statue they say is holy, or a piece of cloth they say is from an altar-cloth, or collect money to build a new church.

Dützbetterings: Beggarwomen who spread a sheet over themselves, and set wax and eggs by them, as tho' they were in childbed, and say their babe died recently. Some say they have given birth to a child and a live toad.

Gickisses: Beggars who take cotton, make the cotton bloody, and then with a kerchief tie this over their eyes, and say they were blinded by wicked men in a forest and tied fast to a tree. This is called *broken wandering*.

Grantners: Knaves who pretend to suffer from St. Vitus' dance [falling sickness]. Some place pieces of soap in their mouth, whereby foam rises as big as a fist.

Süntvegers: Women who wander the country, and say that formerly they led a loose life, and that now they repent.

Vopperinae: Women who take a cow's spleen, and peel it on one side, and then lay it upon their bosom—the peeled part outside—besmearing it with blood, in order that people may think it is the breast.

Voppers: These are women who allow themselves to be led in chains as if they were raving mad.

   (**Voppen** = to cheat)

Virgins: Women who carry rattles as though they were real lepers, and yet they are not.

Chapter 3

A PICTURE COMES INTO VIEW

———

Several months after I found my grandfather's article in 1995 and did my initial research into Luther and the history of Rotwelsch, my father came to visit me in Cambridge. I got home late and found him sitting on the stoop of my triple-decker, located on a dead-end alley called Caldwell Avenue—"I see, an avenue in the grand European tradition," a friend joked. The alley was always full of trash because on the corner lived an old man who spent his time drinking Bud Light and tossing the empty cans into the alley. His son liked trash even more. When the garbage truck came, he helped by grabbing trash cans and throwing them as high as he could, scattering their contents everywhere.

My father didn't seem to mind the mess. I took him to an Irish pub around the corner, the Druid, which I knew he would like because he had spent time in Scotland and Ireland. The boisterous atmosphere wasn't ideal for what promised to be a trying conversation; perhaps I hoped that the noise would distract us.

The Druid was crowded, but as soon as we were each holding a pint, I blurted out my discovery: "You never told me that
Grandpa hated Jews!" He looked completely surprised, almost
uncomprehending. "What?" He made me repeat what I had
said. "Martin, don't say that." He was looking around, panicked,
fearing that people had overheard. But the Druid was loud, and
we were speaking in German. Once, he had told me that when
he was hanging out in pubs in Ireland, people had expressed
their approval of Hitler for attacking England, but I doubted
that my father was thinking of that now. I kept at it. "I found an
article, from 1934, in which Grandpa attacked Jews for hiding
behind false names. Did you know about this?" He was clearly
confused. "Martin, of course I didn't. Where did you find it?"
"In the library. It's the greatest library in the world," I added,
sarcastically. My father stuttered: "But Grandpa only wrote
about obscure names." "Not in this case, he didn't. I guess none
of you ever bothered to check." "Check his articles? Why would
we?" Finally, I added: "He even attacked Rotwelsch."

My father fell silent. Looking into his drink, he mumbled
that he didn't know about any of it. I tried to catch his eye and
gave up. For a while, we listened to the noise of the bar. My
father twisted his mustache, which he did when he didn't know
what to say, two quick deliberate movements with thumb and
index finger. Then he looked up and turned around, as if to see
whether people were following our conversation, which they
still weren't, and swallowed hard a couple of times. As a kid, I
had been fascinated by his large Adam's apple, which was working overtime now, moving up and down dramatically. After
looking around the pub one last time, he told me a story I had
never heard before.

Shortly before I was born, after my parents had moved out

of the commune, my father had taken up photography and got a kit for his birthday so that he could develop his own images. Pleased with his new hobby, he had decided to make a calendar of old family photos and asked his mother for negatives. One of the negatives captured a particularly nice family scene. His mother is sitting outside with her older child (my uncle) on her lap at a round table with a white tablecloth. A handwritten note at the bottom says that it is June 1937, a year before my father was born. There are two pieces of bread on the table, a knife, and a plate with a large, white radish. My grandfather is smiling, though little gaps between his teeth make him look slightly scary. He is making his one-year-old lick foam from a glass of beer (standard child-rearing practice in Bavaria even today). "Maybe that's why we like to drink," my father added, attempting to laugh.

My father told me how he projected the enlarged negative onto photographic paper, then placed the paper in the tray with the developing agent and watched the image slowly take

shape. As the photo developed, my father noticed that my grand-father was wearing a button on his jacket, a round white button that was a little difficult to make out. Interested, my father got a magnifying glass and managed to see it quite clearly. It was a *zinken* of a very particular sort: a swastika.

"I immediately called Günter—he didn't know either," my father said. "We really tore into Iha," he added, using their child-hood name for their father. "Iha" was how German expresses the neighing of a horse; the name must have emerged when their father would carry them around on his back, pretending to be a horse. "We were shocked and really mad at him." He looked me in the eye at last: "Well, now you know." He had lapsed into a Bavarian dialect, which he did when he was agitated.

Similar scenes to the one between my father, his brother, and their father were happening all around Germany in the 1960s, as a younger generation discovered secrets and half-suppressed knowledge, breaking the era of silence and amnesia that had descended upon Germany in the decades immediately following the war. True, there had been some reckoning with the worst Nazi crimes immediately after the war, during the Nuremberg trials, when twenty of the worst offenders were convicted. Follow-up trials had focused on particular profes-sions, including law and medicine, and yielded some additional convictions, but by the end of the 1940s, the political will for large-scale punishment had given way to new realities. The western part of Germany was becoming an important ally of the United States, Great Britain, and France in the Cold War, and all energy was now devoted to rebuilding the bombed-out country. Most former Nazis were able to continue in their old professions through the fifties and early sixties without too much difficulty.

Things began to change as my father's generation came of age and questioned the postwar consensus of not asking too many questions. While in America the generational struggle of the sixties was about civil rights and the Vietnam War, in Germany it was about former Nazis who, having escaped scrutiny, were still in positions of power. The conflict tore families apart along generational lines.

After he was done with his story in the Druid, my father sketched the uproar that ensued, the heated conversations between the brothers as they demanded explanations. "Iha" responded by saying that he had done nothing wrong, that they didn't know what they were talking about, that it was only a button, nothing else. He was irascible, like his sons. I'm sure it was quite a scene, with lots of shouting and neighing.

Strangely, my father didn't say anything about the reactions of his sister, Roswitha. More than a decade younger, she would have been in her late teens at the time, certainly old enough to be told something or perhaps even participate in the generational reckoning. Why was she left out? My father described it purely as something between the two brothers and their Iha.

Then something strange happened between my father, his brother, and their swastika-wearing father: nothing. The shocking discovery was allowed to drift into the background. It was their mother who persuaded them to let the matter rest. "Leave the old man alone," she said about her husband, who was then sixty-one years old. There was no more talk about it at all. A great silence descended, and my father never thought of mentioning it to me as I was growing up and reaching adulthood.

After my father had finished telling me this story, we both

felt completely spent. I don't remember what else we talked about—probably not much. The next day, he wanted to look at some buildings, since he was in town with a group of architecture students. We walked around Cambridge and he pointed out to me some of the city's important landmarks, mostly buildings at MIT and Harvard. Then he needed to catch up with his charges. He left behind his architectural guide, with handwritten marginal notes. It is what I now associate with this visit, and I sometimes take it out to remember not so much the buildings as the conversation we had the day before.

Why had he never told me? This wasn't how historical reckoning was supposed to work. I had learned a lot about the Holocaust in school, as Germany, reluctantly and belatedly, had developed a culture of coming to terms with the past in the 1970s and '80s. (Of course, there was a single word for the whole phrase, *Vergangenheitsbewältigung*, far from the quick one and two syllables of Rotwelsch.) The past was supposed to be out in the open now, in textbooks, in the conduct of the entire nation, in its reluctance to engage in new wars, and in its support of Israel. And it was. My generation grew up studying the Third Reich quite thoroughly, at least those of us who graduated from high school. The country also devoted itself to remembering its sins through school trips to concentration camps. I still recall those visits and the effects they had on us viscerally. One girl in our class vomited outside the gates of Dachau. In the school bus going home, we were quiet.

Germany's reckoning with the past took place largely without Jews. In my class, there was a single Israeli girl, painfully shy, who was visibly uncomfortable in this group of Germans making their awkward attempts to deal with the Nazi past. I remember one moment when she asserted herself. We were learning the opening of Genesis in Hebrew. We hadn't studied the language, but our teacher thought we should be able to recite the opening lines in the original. I still remember them: *"B-re'shiyt bara Elohim 'et hashamayim v'et ha'aretz. Veha'arets hayetah tohu vavohu"* (In the beginning God created the heaven and the earth. And the earth was without form and void). I soaked up those words, ancient and resonant, about the creation of the world.

The problem was that none of us, including the teacher, knew how to pronounce these words. So, this painfully shy girl, about ten years old, got up on her own initiative and without being called on just started to say them out loud, with unusual confidence, ending with the last ringing *tohu vavohu*, the word for formlessness, chaos. From then on, *tohu vavohu* became a word we used all the time, in all kinds of situations. I have a distinct image of chaos evoked by this word. It's a liquid mess *vavohuing* around, bubbling and bursting with sudden explosions of *tohu: tohu vavohu*. Yes, that's what chaos should be called. The Israeli girl left at the end of the year. In her honor, we collected funds to have olive trees planted in Israel.

The other time when history lessons about the Third Reich took on a visceral quality was when we listened to Hitler's voice, the screeching and hysterical speeches that seemed to us closer to Charlie Chaplin's nonsense imitation than what a real human could sound like. It was difficult to connect this clown to the horrors we had learned about in our textbooks. One of my classmates took to barking Hitler speeches during recess, a reaction to the combination of horror and comedy we saw in those strange performances. It wasn't that we weren't taking this lesson seriously. We just didn't know how to respond to something that was unthinkable and absurd.

Despite such parodies, we embraced the task of remembering our country's misdeeds. For me, reckoning with the Holocaust became the main reason for studying history. I needed to know and understand how it happened in order to prevent it from happening again, both in Germany and elsewhere. Knowing history, for me, became a moral imperative. (East Germany dealt with the past differently: many Communists had been in the Resistance during the Nazi era, and after the war East Germany regarded itself as a new country, without the obligation to take responsibility for what had come before.)

A strange word: *Vergangenheitsbewältigung*. Strictly speaking, it doesn't mean coming to terms with the past but something closer to accomplishing history in the sense of completing a task, getting it done, overcoming it, as if the past were a problem that could be solved and be done with. Perhaps this is why the consensus about this policy is fraying now: the term promised that reckoning with the past would be accomplished soon, if only enough dedication were brought to it. But now it looks like there won't ever be an end to it, that the past isn't something that will ever go away.

I don't remember that I ever asked my parents point-blank what my grandparents had done during the 1930s and '40s. All I knew was that they were both "in the war" and that my maternal grandfather had been killed. Why didn't I ask for details? Because something as unthinkable as the Holocaust happened elsewhere, in a past unconnected to me and those dear to me. We were living in a different universe, the 1980s. We were worried about a revival of the Cold War (I was living within ninety miles of the Iron Curtain), and we were culturally oriented toward the United States. What could the drab and dreary images of unspeakable suffering from the 1930s and '40s have in common with stonewashed jeans and perms? If there was silence, I was complicit in it, helping this secret to be passed down from one generation to the next.

Yet the past had left a trace, a symbol, a *zinken*, and my father had dragged the past out from hiding by finding it and deciphering it. Through this discovery, he and his brother had to create a new story of their parentage and their inheritance— which they did, while still keeping good relations with their father. Then, I rediscovered the past all over again, through another accident; this time in an article found buried in a faraway library, an article about Rotwelsch and Jewish names.

The state-sanctioned regime of commemoration, so exemplary in many ways, wasn't enough, or perhaps it had simply been too impersonal, appropriate to studying causes and circumstances of remote periods but not something closer to home, something that is home. History, even when it deals with the actions of people, tends to be distant and can therefore be absorbed without putting yourself, your own person, on the line. Family history is different: it challenges the instinct within families to keep things hidden, the desire to spare children from harmful knowledge about their parents or grandparents, the desire of children to love their parents despite what they might have done.

Studying history can be motivated by the desire to prevent it from repeating itself, out there in the world. The story of your family goes deeper and affects the sense of who you are and where you come from; it goes to the very core of your being. Perhaps my grandfather had had a sense of that when he studied family names and family histories.

I didn't articulate these notions very clearly in my mind after the confrontation with my father at the Druid. My thoughts at the time were confused, jumbled together, as I tried to force together the two: capital-H history and my family's past. I had recently moved to America, more or less on a fluke, and was enjoying the sense of possibility and openness that came with my new surroundings. I had arrived here at a good moment, when America was looking toward a bright future. The Cold War had ended, and the internet was promising all kinds of utopian and commercial possibilities. I soaked it all up. A friend was developing something called "e-paper" in a lab near MIT and kept telling me that the invention, once it worked, would transform the world. Hoping to be part of this new movement, I applied for a job at a computer startup, only to find that as a foreign student on a visa, I didn't have the right work permit. But I was undeterred. America was moving into the future and somehow, I was going to be part of it.

Several times I wanted to pick up the phone and call my father, only to decide that such topics were best reserved for face-to-face conversation, preferably in a noisy pub while downing a couple of pints. I postponed that talk to the next time I would see him.

I never got a chance to have that conversation. A few months after our meeting at the Druid, I received a telephone call from my department, telling me to call a number in Germany that I didn't recognize. My mother was on the line and explained that she was staying at a lake near Munich, and that my father was dead.

My father and my two brothers had been sailing. They were

caught by a storm and the boat capsized. They were all wearing life vests, but my father had gotten entangled in ropes and been dragged underwater. My brothers tried to get him out but failed. Eventually, a boat came, they cut him free and brought him to land, but all attempts to revive him were unsuccessful. He was fifty-eight, which seemed old to me at the time. A full life, I foolishly told myself. I was twenty-six.

The months following were turmoil and chaos. Because my father had died so suddenly, his estate was in complete disarray. At first, I went through his papers almost randomly, finding documents connected to our house, his various professional activities, and to his sister, Roswitha, whom he had helped in various ways. A multimillion-dollar lawsuit against my father's small architectural firm had been going on for years, and my father's partner, whom he had brought into the firm, now claimed that the whole thing had been my father's fault. I spent weeks going through the firm's papers and was able to establish the partner's culpability. But in the end, none of it mattered. To shield the family from the claims of the partner and the looming lawsuit, I had to declare my father's estate insolvent. Two months after my father's death, my inheritance disappeared.

But my father's true legacy was only beginning. Among his business correspondence and papers, I found many poems that he had written over the years. They were both dark and loving. One, very short, was a pun on the similarity in sound, in German, of the words for smart and failed (*gescheit/gescheitert*): "Smart at twenty / Smarter at forty / Outsmarted at sixty." He was contemplating his own failure—although I didn't know in what sense. Externally, his life had been a success: a family; a thriving architectural practice; a professorship at the technical university. What had he been seeking, in the middle of the night, in March 1995, when he wrote this short poem, a little over a year before his death? Why was he worried about what would happen to him at sixty, an age he would in fact never reach?

It occurred to me that March '95 was just around the time when he had visited me in Cambridge and I had confronted him with my discovery about his father. Was it this conversation that had forced him to raise, once again, the question of his own position in the world?

A second poem written around the same time seemed to hint at an answer:

> I wanted to
> inscribe my life for you
> into the sand of the river,
> with the bow of the violin,
> into the mountain ranges
> and the furrow of the trail.
>
> The edge of the forest
> clearly bears my signature.
> Later, when you interpret it,
> fill the violin with sand—
> and listen
> to the movement of the grains.

He is speaking in the past tense of what he wanted to do, namely leave traces for us, messages that he tried to inscribe into the landscape. He knew that we would be searching for him, for his life, after his death. He was right. It is what I have been doing ever since.

My father taught me how to play the violin when I was seven years old and the instrument bound us together. We sometimes fought when playing, but now I think about these sessions often.

The poem also reminded me of those hiking trips from my early childhood when I would be looking for *zinken* inscribed by wandering Rotwelsch speakers on the side of the road. We would stay at village inns or monasteries, which were often unheated, and we hiked in all kinds of weathers, not like the fair-weather hikers my father derided. The inns were smoky and the bars frequented by local farmers and loggers. They would be playing cards or an archaic game that involved driving large nails into a log with a single stroke of the hammer.

What kept me from complaining on those hikes was the prospect of finding hidden travelers' signs. My father had a good eye for them and would point out the runes left by travelers by the side of the road or on houses and barns. Isolated farmhouses, which were called *Einöden*, the German word for desolation, were the best candidates for these signs, but *Einöden* were often fiercely guarded by aggressive dogs. Before approaching such a place, my father would tell me to find a walking stick for self-defense. More often than not, we needed one. Once, after I had been frightened by a particularly nasty dog, my father pointed out the sign, carved into a nearby tree: it looked like two *W*s in a row: WW. A Rotwelsch speaker had come by here and warned other travelers about the dog, whose fletched teeth the sign imitated.

But only now, as I was learning more about these *zinken*, did I fully appreciate how profound they were. They were left behind, like my father's poem and the message he had inscribed into the landscape and the furrow of the road, for others to read in the future. These tramps, often on the verge of starvation, were helping others with useful hints. Their signatures were even more intriguing. They weren't useful, either to themselves or others, but they were an attempt to leave a trace of a life that had existed at a particular point and at a particular time. "The edge of the forest bears my signature," my father had written. A life inscribed onto the world for those who have eyes to read it.

When I wasn't researching my father's professional activities or reading his poems, I would visit his grave, which was located in the most beautiful cemetery of the city. The gravestones were made of sandstone and placed horizontally on the ground. Because of the sandy soil, the cemetery was full of roses. The graves of Nuremberg's most famous citizens lay here, from a time when the city had been a cultural center, home of the painter Albrecht Dürer and other Renaissance artists and intellectuals. The beauty of the cemetery and the graves of these people attracted busloads of tourists, but fortunately my father's grave was off to one side, away from the famous dead.

Over the next couple of months, the heavy gravestone would start to sink into the earth, as the coffin and its contents began to disintegrate. My mother had planted a rosebush in front of his grave, and the rosebush was thriving. At one point I was filled with an irrational rage against this plant, which blithely transformed a rotting corpse into fragrant flowers.

Distracted by the roses, I talked to my father, reporting to him on the progress of my investigation of his business, the betrayal of his partner, and how we had to declare his estate insolvent. I hoped he didn't mind. I told him it was for the best of the family.

During these conversations the unresolved question of Rotwelsch surfaced again. The language was mysteriously connected to our family, and there were questions I wanted to ask him, about his father, about his discovery of the swastika on the lapel, about why he had remained silent. I also wanted to tell him about Rotwelsch and anti-Semitism, and how his father fit into a long tradition of those attacking Rotwelsch and its speakers. I wondered whether my father had known something of this history from his brother, and whether he cared.

ROTWELSCH LESSON:

HOW TO DIE IN ROTWELSCH

Abmecken = to do someone in; to kill

Ausmecken = to delete, kill (*mocho* means eradicate)

Kürbiszupf = beheading (literally squash-zupf)

Krachen gehen = to die (to go crash)

Chajess lekichnen = to take a life (*chai* means life)

Flattern = to die; also *flattermoss*, a woman who washes the dead (*fladern*, to wash)

Galgel = a breaking wheel (*galgal* means wheel)

Hargenen = to murder someone (*horeg* means murderer)

Heimschicker = murderer (literally, someone who sends people home)

Kaporen = to kill (*kapore* means prepared for sacrifice in the temple)

Ketel = murder

Krachen = to be arrested; to die

Tabboch = butcher (*tevakh* means to slaughter animals)

Verschwarzen = to die

Tot sein (literally, to be dead) = an expression that means to have no money

Also Useful

Schiwe = mourning (*shive*, seven, as in the prescribed seven
   days of mourning)
Kewer = grave (*kever*, grave)

Chapter 4

THE ROTWELSCH INHERITANCE

My aunt Heidi, Günter's widow, had trouble finding the right boxes, as she moved erratically around the attic, trying to read labels. Then she crouched down in a corner and said, quietly, "Here they are. Take your time." She briefly looked at me as if to gauge my reaction, and left, eager to go back downstairs. I stood for a moment, disappointed. Just a bunch of boxes. The labels, carelessly scrawled with Magic Marker, were illegible.

I had come to the apartment that used to house the commune to find out more about Rotwelsch, my uncle, and his attitude toward his father. Three people had been around at the time and could tell me more. The first was my mother, but in the aftermath of my father's death, she was holding things together from one day to the next and was in no condition to delve into the past. I knew that I would have to wait to speak to her.

Then there was my aunt Roswitha. She would have been a teenager when Günter became fascinated by Rotwelsch, but perhaps she would have some insight, an overheard conversation ages ago about her older brother and his new interest, a snide comment about Rotwelsch made by my grandfather. I would have to find an occasion to draw her out. And finally there was Heidi, the person most likely to know things about Günter, Rotwelsch, and the strange family history connected with it, which is why I had come to her first.

I dragged one box into the middle of the attic, where a small window let in some light. It contained folders of correspondence and manuscripts as well as books. The next three boxes were similar, but then I came across one holding 4-x-6 index cards, neatly arranged in wooden drawers. I took one drawer out, surprised by how heavy it was, and started flipping through the entries. The cards—there must have been hundreds of them—bore expressions and idioms, most of them typed, some corrected by hand. The last box, equally heavy, held dictionaries of Romani and Yiddish, pamphlets on hoboes and vagrants. They had seen a lot of use, their spines cracked and their covers coming off the binding. One book, almost torn to shreds, was entitled *Rotwelsch*. Yes, this was what I had been looking for: my uncle's fabled Rotwelsch archive.

Combing quickly through the boxes, I saw that this was an archive that, at least superficially, looked similar to archives created by the police *against* Rotwelsch, complete with vocabulary lists, names of vagrants, and police records. I was fascinated by the figures that emerged from this extensive collection. Here were the ancestors of the people who had come to our house when I was growing up—escaped convicts, runaway apprentices, deserters, itinerant peddlers, tramps, professional thieves, beggars, hoboes, journeymen, knife grinders, tinkers, migrants, and anyone at odds with the authorities and without a fixed address. Some members of the underground were organized into large gangs of robbers, especially in the eighteenth century. They would send a messenger, a *baldower*, to scout out a promising target (in Hebrew, *baal* means possessor, owner, and *davar*, word; in Yiddish, *bal-dover* means the person in question). Once the leader had received enough information to proceed, he (almost always men) would call for a gathering of his associates, the *kochemer*, or wise ones, to plan the robbery.

Short summer nights weren't ideal, and snow made it difficult to get away quickly, which meant that long, moonless nights in the spring or the fall were best. The gang would split into small groups to infiltrate the area and then meet up at a prearranged point. Usually they would sneak up on their target or else walk openly into a village singing French songs, pretending they were French soldiers looking for a good time. If they met anyone along the way who made trouble, members of the gang would tie them up and leave them on the side of the road. If he felt cocky, the gang leader would march at the head of the column, ceremoniously holding a crowbar like a scepter, approach the targeted house, and break down the door. The inhabitants would be bound and forced to reveal where they kept their valuables. If the *baldower* had exaggerated their possessions, the family was in a tough spot and needed to produce the expected goods somehow, though gangs usually avoided bloodshed. After the goods were discovered and collected, a code word would alert everyone to meet in front of the house and beat a hasty retreat, which often meant a forced march lasting several hours. When they had put enough distance between themselves and their victims, they would stop, divvy up the loot according to rank and function, and go on their separate ways.

Planning and executing a robbery of this magnitude, and keeping discipline among outlaws, was difficult, even more so to keep successful heists secret afterward. Concealment was everything. To avoid detection, gang members would blacken or otherwise conceal their faces during the robbery. Once the victims had given up their hidden valuables, they would be covered with their own bedsheets so they couldn't observe what was going on. Code names and passwords offered additional protection.[1]

In addition to these measures, robbers had developed their secret language precisely so that they could speak in front of victims or bystanders undetected. So highly regarded was this language that some of the largest gangs deliberately added words to it and sent out emissaries to other regions to make sure that the new words were widely used. They knew that Rotwelsch was their most valuable weapon against the authorities and were eager to perfect it. Parents beat children until they stopped using the standard language and spoke exclusively in Rotwelsch.[2]

Sometimes, the speakers called this language not *Rot-welsch* (beggar's cant), the pejorative word used by most people, but *kochemer loshn* (in Hebrew, *khokhem* means a wise person and *loshn*, tongue, or language): the language of those in the know; the lingo of the wise guys. This insider talk created a bond among the outcasts because it distinguished those who belonged to the road from those who didn't, the wise ones from the know-nothings.

A notorious member of this underclass was a woman called Grinder Berbel. Like many women of the itinerant underground, Grinder Berbel often worked as a *baldower*, scouting out possible targets for robberies (other women would act as market thieves or smuggle tools to prison inmates to help them escape). If Berbel couldn't communicate with a gang directly, she would use elaborate *zinken* to mark a target and to communicate other essential information. A *zinken* might even include information about when the robbery would take place.[3]

Even though Berbel was married to a knife grinder, hence her name Grinder Berbel, she had other lovers, and this led to frequent physical fights with other women. By all accounts, she was an unusually strong and willful woman who did as she pleased.

This attitude led her into a liaison with the much younger Konstanzer Hans. Born Johann Baptist Herrenberger (1759–1793), Konstanzer Hans had drifted into the underground in his teens. Grinder Berbel inducted him into the higher echelons of robbery, including Rotwelsch and *zinken*, skills that Hans ultimately parleyed into an illustrious career as a thief. He would become one of the most notorious robbers of the eighteenth century, earning him the street name Konstanzer Hans.

Grinder Berbel and Konstanzer Hans preferred to rob civil servants and other representatives of the state, guaranteeing them support from the poor. This did not help Hans when he had the misfortune of falling into the hands of an experienced detective, Jacob Georg Schäffer, in 1782.[4] Schäffer wasn't

A thief known for speaking many languages (parrot) plans a robbery (key) in a church on St. Stephanus Day, i.e., December 26 (the three stones: St. Stephanus was martyred by stoning). To this purpose, he or she will meet willing collaborators here, at the location of this *zinken*, on Christmas Day (infant).

fooled by Hans's forged documents and aliases but still needed to prove the identity of his catch. Cunningly, he arrested Hans's father. Usually the father would help his son—in one instance, he and Hans had exchanged secret information in Rotwelsch in front of a judge—but the two had recently quarreled and the father, now worried about being implicated in the son's crimes, identified Hans in court. Hans was stunned and protested that he didn't know the old man, but to no avail.

Forced to confess, Hans revealed an entire underworld of crime, including safe houses, secret meeting places, and the identities of more than five hundred criminals, in addition to a small dictionary of Rotwelsch words.[5] For centuries, the police had been trying to decode Rotwelsch, prying these secret words out of its speakers, word by word, captive by captive. Hans's confession provided a breakthrough. Instead of going down in history as a latter-day Robin Hood, he became a turncoat who gave the police crucial insight into the secret language of thieves.

Hans was only one of many Rotwelsch speakers whose stories emerged from the archive, but his story was embellished and published by hacks for a broad market. Konstanzer Hans had been popular, and his tale was too, especially since it was couched in a moralizing tone, "written as a warning," a note said, which meant that upright burghers could enjoy the tale of this outlaw without qualms.[6]

There was little information in my uncle's archive about the ultimate fate of Grinder Berbel. Apparently Hans had abandoned her, refusing to help his former lover and teacher when she was arrested and imprisoned; perhaps they had quarreled again and Hans had decided to make a clean break. Rumors emerged she hanged herself in prison. Other sources reported that she was freed and continued with her colorful life until well into her seventies.[7] If she lived to that ripe age, unusual for someone constantly on the road, she would have had plenty of time to regret what she had taught Konstanzer Hans, one of the greatest *molsamers* (traitors) of the underground.

=====

After looking through my uncle's boxes, I asked Aunt Heidi about Rotwelsch. We were sitting in the old-fashioned kitchen, which hadn't been renovated since the days of the commune. My aunt lit a cigarette and looked at me, but she was reluctant to talk about Günter and Rotwelsch. I knew that he had studied music, had become an accomplished pianist, and had started to make a name for himself as a composer. One of his compositions, an oratorio, had been performed by a well-known orchestra and broadcast on national public radio (at my father's funeral, my brother Stephan had selected one of Günter's compositions to be played). All this was before Günter caught the Rotwelsch bug and devoted himself more or less exclusively to researching the language.

It occurred to me that I had always taken my uncle's single-minded study of Rotwelsch for granted, unaware that there was something odd, something mysterious and troubling that might require an explanation. I had never asked myself why he had given up on music. What had he hoped to achieve by studying Rotwelsch? And what were the costs of his fascination?

My aunt took one of the handwritten Rotwelsch dictionaries out of my hand and waved it in front of my face. "Do you know who made this?" "Uncle Günter?" I said. "Wrong. I did. He would dictate to me night after night, and I had to write everything down, dead tired because I was also bringing up your three cousins."

I had always regarded my family's infatuation with Rotwelsch as a male affair, something my uncle had taught me and that I had traced to his father. Now I was beginning to see that women played a central role. My aunt Heidi had been a reluctant collaborator in my uncle's life project, just as my mother had interacted with vagrants drawn to our house by a Rotwelsch *zinken*. I made a mental note to approach my other aunt, Roswitha. What had she known of her father's past and her brother's dedication to a thieves' language that her father had hoped to eliminate?

Meanwhile the boxes were upstairs and my aunt sat across from me. I had a million questions for her. Above all, I wanted to hear about the strange relationship between my grandfather's hatred for Rotwelsch and my uncle's dedication to it: "Did my uncle and his father ever fight about Rotwelsch?" "No. Why would they?" The thought seemed never to have occurred to her, and I didn't have the heart to tell her why I was asking. But it was clear that Rotwelsch was a highly charged matter even after all these years.

Pointing upstairs, to the attic, she said: "You can have it all. I don't need it anymore. Take it."

This was how I came into possession of my uncle's Rotwelsch archive. (My cousins also agreed to let me have the archive.) I shipped it to Massachusetts, where I could sift through it more carefully, hoping to learn not only about Rotwelsch but also about why my uncle was so drawn to the language. The archive contained my uncle's manuscripts and correspondence, his field notes, his index cards full of Rotwelsch expressions and idioms, his published work, and books he had collected (some of which my aunt kept, not wanting to leave Rotwelsch behind entirely after all).

I felt sure that my uncle's archive was the key. But the key to what? I have now been dragging this archive around with me for twenty-five years, and I read around in it when I can't sleep at night, when I think about the past, when I miss my father. I have come to think of it as my other inheritance, the one that didn't end in bankruptcy: my Rotwelsch inheritance.

══

Initially, the archive didn't say much about my uncle or my father, but it took me deep into the history of Rotwelsch. By the time Martin Luther published his *Liber Vagatorum*, Rotwelsch had already been around for hundreds of years. The earliest sighting of the term dated to CE 1250, when the term Rotwelsch was used to describe deceptions, a usage that dovetailed with my grandfather's coinage of so-called camouflage names almost seven hundred years later.

My uncle's archive revealed something else: the Hebrew terms, which Luther had taken as proof that Rotwelsch "comes from the Jews," were there primarily because of Yiddish. My uncle had spent considerable time reconstructing the story of this Germanic language spoken by Jewish communities. When my grandfather had made a connection between Yiddish and Rotwelsch, however hate filled, he was not entirely wrong.

The story of Yiddish was a story of migration. Future Yiddish speakers arrived in western Germany from France and Italy during the early Middle Ages, speaking a distinct version of Old French and Old Italian. Once they settled in the western part of Germany, and then established outposts along the Danube, they adopted German as the language of everyday communication. Hebrew was used in the context of the Bible and its interpretation, a *loshn koydesh*, or sacred language (as opposed to the Rotwelsch *kochemer loshn*, the language of those in the know).[8]

But what kind of German was it? Because Jewish settlers lived in distinct communities (though not yet in ghettos), their version of German was different from that spoken around them. It contained words specific to Jewish life, from kosher foods to religious institutions as well as phrases and expressions useful to the specific needs of these communities. This early Yiddish would have been a variant of Middle High German, the German preserved in medieval epics.

Life for these settlers became harder with the Crusades, which recruited soldiers to liberate the holy land by whipping up anti-Semitic sentiments across Western Europe. These campaigns of hate laid the foundation for a second wave of anti-Semitism prompted by the arrival of the plague in 1348. Desperate populations were looking for scapegoats, and the Jewish communities, already branded as foreign, became convenient candidates. Faced with increasing persecution, German-speaking Jewish communities in Central Europe, a territory they called Ashkenaz, found themselves driven east and settling in Eastern Europe. Surrounded by speakers of Slavic languages, these migrants stuck to their distinct form of German. While the German spoken in Germany evolved from Middle High German into Modern German, in part through the efforts of writers such as Luther, the language preserved in these eastern Jewish communities continued on its own path, slowly becoming a distinct tongue.[9] Its speakers mostly referred to their language as *taytsh* (German), *yidish-taytsh* (Jewish German), or *undzer loshn* (our language). Only toward the end of that process, in the nineteenth century, was that language routinely labeled as Yiddish (which simply means Jewish), a shortening of *yidish-taytsh*.

=====

A third set of boxes in my uncle's archive contained material on generations of policemen who had tried to decrypt Rotwelsch, colleagues of Schäffer, the detective who had hunted Konstanzer Hans. I was skeptical of these policemen, the natural enemies of Rotwelsch, in league with Rotwelsch haters such as Luther. Luther was part of a large-scale attack on vagrants as more and more towns, municipalities, and countries passed laws and directives against them. Each person now had to have "papers," as Luther had demanded, different types of permission to pass through lands, to be on the road, to seek apprenticeships, or to work as a peddler. Large, territorial nation-states, created by the Peace of Westphalia, asserted their authority and secured their borders. Not having the required papers meant being vulnerable to arrest and punishment. Being a vagrant, not having a fixed address, was becoming illegal. This was why there were dozens and dozens of Rotwelsch words for prison, including school, sugar house, hell, box, hungry tower, potato palace, and paradise (having a life sentence was called "sky blue," presumably because you remained in prison until ascending to heaven).

There were even more Rotwelsch words for police, in part because there didn't exist a single thing called police, only a patchwork of forces ranging from palace guards and arms-bearing aristocrats to night watchmen, soldiers hired by local rulers to keep the peace, and all kinds of auxiliary forces of law and order. And yet, despite this patchwork, various local police departments had, over time, assembled the record on Rotwelsch that was now sitting in the boxes of my uncle's archive.

Not only were these hostile policemen writing down all kinds of things about Rotwelsch; they were the only ones doing it. Rotwelsch itself was purely a spoken language (except for a few dozen *zinken*). Its speakers didn't need to write it down; in fact, many didn't know how to read and write. The world of the road, from the Middle Ages deep into modern times, did not favor literacy.

The oral nature of Rotwelsch was understandable, given its function. No one felt that it was a problem that Rotwelsch was not written down, except for the unintended consequence that the entire written record on Rotwelsch was therefore written by its enemies, people like Luther and my grandfather who wanted it eliminated. And producing a record of this language, for most of them, was precisely the way in which they wanted to eliminate it. Writing things down, fixing words and names, registering vagrants: all these were connected.

I was becoming suspicious of archives. My grandfather was an archivist. I could see him in my mind's eye working hand in hand with the police. How could I ever hope to understand Rotwelsch through such tainted documents?

There was one policeman I encountered through my uncle's notes who seemed different: Friedrich Christian Benedict Avé-Lallemant (1809–1892). Of French extraction, Avé-Lallemant grew up in an impressive family.[10] Two of his brothers became successful merchants in Brazil, a third had a Tchaikovsky symphony dedicated to him, another, a singer, attracted the attention of the celebrated writer Johann Wolfgang von Goethe, and a fifth became a famous explorer and author. Friedrich chose a different path. After gaining a Ph.D. in law, he joined the police, but he quickly found much to criticize. Living at a time when the first modern police forces were emerging in Germany, he analyzed the influence of the social environment on crime, attacked the criminal justice system as antiquated, and argued for prison reform. He became an advocate for modern criminology.

In his spare time, Avé-Lallemant published novels that portray police corruption and ineptitude—and also the sending and decoding of secret messages. He devoted a book of nonfiction to the topic as well. Given these activities, it is perhaps not surprising that Avé-Lallemant became interested in the secret language of the underground. He, too, wrote as a policeman, but as a modern policeman who wanted to understand this itinerant milieu from a "social-political" vantage point, as he put it in the subtitle of his three-volume tome, which also promised to pay particular attention to the "literary and linguistic" aspects of the underground.[11] He was the first to study the history of Rotwelsch, its grammar, its uses, and the people who spoke it, with something approaching scientific rigor. This didn't mean that he was on their side; but it meant that his observations could be taken as something more than propaganda.

Avé-Lallemant confirmed the view of Rotwelsch as a strange mixture of German, Yiddish, and Hebrew. He noticed that these itinerants were adept at *schmusen*, a word borrowed from the Yiddish *shmooze*, "to converse," but among Rotwelsch speakers it meant speaking Rotwelsch. A prison was a *schul*, an ironic twist on the Yiddish term *shul*, meaning a religious school. Vagrants might be caught by a *schlamasse*, a "policeman," adapted from the Yiddish *shlmazi*, meaning unlucky. Truly, for the *shiksas* (Yiddish for non-Jewish women, in Rotwelsch any women) of the road, encountering a *schlamasse* could only mean bad luck. Vagrants had borrowed Yiddish words, just as they had borrowed German words, and changed their meanings.

But Avé-Lallemant also recognized that some Rotwelsch terms derived from different, non-Jewish sources, including Czech, Latin (because of itinerant students), French, and Romani, the language spoken by Europe's oldest itinerant groups, the Sinti and Roma. In Europe they were sometimes called Gypsies because they were mistakenly believed to be from Egypt. Since there are no historical documents about the origin of these two related groups, their language is the best source of information about them we have, and that source points toward India. How the Sinti and Roma wandered across Asia to the Balkans and then to Central Europe is not known, but somehow they maintained their cohesion, in part through their language. Even more so than Jewish immigrants, Sinti and Roma were seen, in Europe, as the quintessential wandering peoples.

On the European road, the Sinti and Roma tended to keep to themselves, but clearly, they must have interacted with Rotwelsch speakers. In order to track this mysterious influence, Avé-Lallemant befriended a Roma woman, who helped him detect many Romani words in Rotwelsch, such as *hachner* for farmer, after the Romani *hacho*.[12] The association made sense since both groups, Roma and Rotwelsch speakers, were chased from district to district, country to country, always violating the modern world order based on fixed settlement and borders. For all their differences, they shared a common experience, and that commonality led to an exchange of words.

In many ways, Avé-Lallemant did what generations of policemen had done before him: he decrypted a criminal language. Rotwelsch had shown up in studies of ciphers and decryption, as well as in manuals on how best to send secret messages through code, and he continued that tradition. As a policeman, he regarded Rotwelsch as a hostile force, a weapon that needed to be disarmed.

But I sensed something else in Avé-Lallemant's writing: a certain understanding for the people of the road. Perhaps his second identity as a writer (and as a critic of police corruption) helped him empathize with Rotwelsch speakers and appreciate their wit. But the most important feature was his lifelong passion for language itself, for Rotwelsch. He was more than a policeman, and something closer to a linguist. He correctly identified Rotwelsch as a sociolect, the lexicon of a distinct subgroup, and he wanted to understand it and the world from which it had emerged. Avé-Lallemant approached Rotwelsch as a historical phenomenon, one that deserved careful and systematic study. (I also learned that underground languages such as Rotwelsch could be found in many parts of the world.)

It is thanks to his studies that the old story of Rotwelsch as a "Jewish" language, promoted by Luther, my grandfather, and many writers in between, has now been effectively disproven. While Yiddish was spoken by an ethnically and religiously identified community, Rotwelsch was not primarily spoken by Jewish vagrants. Both Grinder Berbel and Konstanzer Hans, for example, had grown up in Christian families before drifting into the underground. There might have been some Jewish scouts, or *baldower*, and in the Netherlands there were Jewish gangs that extended their reach into Germany, but Rotwelsch, even if it had partially "come from the Jews," as Luther insisted, was now firmly in the hands of Christians. Or rather, it was used by people who were united not by religion or ethnicity, but by a particular form of life: the life on the road. If Yiddish (and, via Yiddish, Hebrew) played a larger role than the other languages, it was because vagrants would have interacted with Jewish peddlers and Jewish gangs and borrowed from their way of speaking. Perhaps the fact that most Christians wouldn't understand these borrowed terms was a welcome by-product. But there was nothing specifically Jewish about Rotwelsch speakers. The confusion of Rotwelsch and Yiddish was primarily the work of anti-Semites for whom speaking a Jewish-inflected German and speaking a thieves' language was pretty much the same thing.

Avé-Lallemant also confirmed that the mixture of languages present in Rotwelsch was built on a German base. Various German dialects provided the grammar as well as most of the small, grammatical words such as personal pronouns (you, I, they) and prepositions (after, toward). This was why Rotwelsch drove so many people crazy: it *sounded* like German, but was incomprehensible to an outsider.

As I was appreciating all Avé-Lallemant had done for the understanding of Rotwelsch, I wondered whether I had been wrong to think of the police as the enemies of this language. Perhaps the police were just doing their job decrypting an underground language, and Avé-Lallemant had simply taken things one step further. The true enemies were ideologues such as Luther and my grandfather, those driven by anxieties about the mixing of languages and peoples, about the purity of speech and blood. They had turned a police affair—how to deal with vagrants and their words—into a crisis of national importance, using Rotwelsch to spread panic.

Where did this leave my uncle? I tried to remember as many aspects of his life as I could. He was notorious in the family for hanging out in dive bars and other places of ill repute, which I had always chalked up to a kind of bohemian slumming. (My father had similar tendencies, though didn't indulge them quite to the same extent.) But now, while going through the cards and dictionaries from his archive, I wondered whether he had been doing fieldwork, trying to find the last Rotwelsch speakers still alive. Painstakingly, and with the crucial help from his wife, he had filled index cards and dictionaries with Rotwelsch words and expressions. Some he had gathered from sources like Martin Luther and police files on figures such as Grinder Berbel and Konstanzer Hans, but others he had found by chatting up or even befriending low-life characters. I began to see aspects of his life in light of his interest in Rotwelsch. The language was much more than a hobby or the professional interest of a writer: he was obsessed with it.

The only thing I didn't know was why my uncle had become obsessed with this language in the first place, or what my father thought about it, and it was too late to ask them.

=====

As I was going through my uncle's archive looking for answers to these questions, I came across a copy of Hitler's *Mein Kampf.* It had belonged to my grandfather. Why did Günter feel that this book should be part of his Rotwelsch archive? I had never read this book, which, along with swastikas and other Nazi paraphernalia, was forbidden in Germany until 2016.

Once, of course, it had been available everywhere. Hitler had written it while imprisoned for a failed putsch in 1923. The book was long, convoluted, full of details strung together by a skewed theory of history collected from random sources, interlaced with autobiographical fragments. After the Nazi party rose to prominence and seized power, *Mein Kampf* was promoted in what must have been one of the great state-sponsored vanity publishing projects in history and often given by local officials to newlyweds. With the power of a totalitarian state behind it, *Mein Kampf* ended up going through 1031 editions, which amounted to around twelve million copies. Every sixth German owned one.[13] This didn't mean that they read it. Did my grandfather ever read it? His copy certainly looked well worn.

Mein Kampf didn't present itself in the first instance as a treatise on race but as an autobiography of young Adolf growing up in the Austrian provinces and arriving in Vienna without means of support, hoping to gain admission to the arts academy. In Vienna, he found himself confronted with cosmopolitan life and failed miserably in his professional plans. He was clearly overwhelmed by the city, which was then the capital of an empire stretching deep into the Balkans. The diversity of peoples and languages was confusing for Hitler, a feeling he quickly turned into hatred, describing it as a "disgusting mixture of Czechs, Poles, Hungarians, Ruthenians, Serbs, Croats, etc. in between which, as eternal dividers, Jews and Jews again."[14]

It wasn't just the people who overwhelmed—or disgusted—Adolf. It was the languages they spoke. He calls it a "tohuwabohu of languages."[15] Was he aware that he was using a Hebrew term, from the opening of Genesis, one I knew well from school? Was this an attempt at linguistic sarcasm? It is difficult to tell. It's one of the very few Hebrew terms he used. For Hitler, *tohuwabohu* had to be eliminated by imposing a "pure" German and getting rid of those people who used words like that one.

Bracketing what became of him, I even found some of Hitler's travails affecting—for example, his failure at the entrance
exam to the arts academy: he was so naïvely confident that he
would get in. Then came the time of poverty and struggle. He
didn't write about it at great length, but it was clear, even in his
reticence, that this time of hardship was humiliating for him.
But just at the moment when the story was at its most affecting, Hitler would digress into a political rant. He had taught
himself all kinds of facts about history, which he turned into a
half-baked worldview. The themes were always the same: purity
against mixture; Aryan versus Jew; German versus *tohuwabohu*.

During his time in Vienna, Hitler developed the theory that
Jews assumed the language of their hosts to disguise themselves. For Jews, "language is not a means of expressing ideas,
but a means of hiding them."[16] Jews never really speak German;
they fake it. Hitler used the term *mauscheln*, the derogatory
term for speaking Yiddish, which was associated with secrecy.[17]

As with so many other of his ideas, Hitler didn't invent this
idea of Yiddish as a secret language. Such a view had accompanied Yiddish from the beginning. That Yiddish was written
with Hebrew characters, which were not accessible to most
Christians, seemed to confirm this idea. In reality, Yiddish was
simply the dialect of a distinct community of speakers who had
retained their religious and ethnic identity over time, partly
to preserve that identity and partly because the surrounding
Christian culture kept its distance. In a kind of paranoia born
from this suspicion, Christians had started to circulate dictionaries of Yiddish expressions, written in the Roman alphabet,
so that Christians would be in a position to decipher this supposedly secret language. These dictionaries treated Yiddish as
if it were Rotwelsch.[18] Even one of the words for Yiddish, *jar-*

gon, which was borrowed from French (before Yiddish became the standard name for the language), meant incomprehensible. Calling Yiddish *jargon* was like calling the language of vagrants *welsch*.

Hitler wasn't done with his theory of Jewish languages. The first stage was disguise—perhaps this was where my grandfather first got the idea of camouflage names. Then came the second stage, which was world domination. "The Jew" would force mankind to adopt a universal language such as Esperanto to rule more effectively.[19]

Hitler developed his theory of language during a time when he himself was homeless, often without food, and sometimes reduced to begging, spending his nights in homeless shelters. There he befriended other drifters and itinerants, including a Jewish one. Among them was Reinhold Hanisch, who had spent time on the road and in various prisons.[20] In his own account, Hanisch described himself as a wanderer and itinerant artisan who met the hapless young Hitler and took him under his wing. Soon, he was peddling Hitler's painted postcards, which allowed the two of them to live without begging.

After Hitler had become chancellor, it was discovered that Hanisch was selling forged Hitler paintings, trying to profit from his former business partner. Hitler moved to get these pictures out of circulation. When he annexed Austria, he had his henchmen purge the local archives of traces of his work and time in Vienna, including in halfway houses.[21] But Hanisch wasn't so easily deterred, and he published a report on his time with Hitler (it was translated into English and published by *The New Republic* in April 1939).[22]

There were several works on the Viennese variants of Rotwelsch in my uncle's archive. Vienna had developed a distinct form of Rotwelsch, as had other cities such as Berlin and Prague. Even though Rotwelsch had long been a language of the road and of the countryside, it had migrated into the underworld of large cities, spoken precisely in the milieu into which Hanisch and Hitler had drifted. If Hitler didn't encounter Rotwelsch through Hanisch, then he would likely have heard it spoken through any of the hundreds of itinerants with whom he had casual contact, and among whom he had slept every night for two years. Some of these occupants of halfway houses must have exchanged words in the jargon of the road or referred to *zinken* in his presence. Perhaps Hitler even picked up a few words himself, before he spat them out again, at least the ones he could identify—for Hitler, too, was probably unaware how many Rotwelsch expressions had already been absorbed into German.

Increasingly, I couldn't help but read *Mein Kampf* as a struggle against Rotwelsch. While Hitler experienced Vienna as a place of racial and linguistic mixture, he imagined Germany as a place of Aryan purity and Prussian militarism. This was where Hitler would end up, via Munich, in charge of Berlin and the Prussian state. And in 1938 he would return to Vienna and declare, triumphantly, "the incorporation of my homeland into the German Reich." At that moment, he also began the "purification" of Vienna, the purging of his homeland of the multicultural mixture the Habsburg Empire had created. I felt that I finally understood just how much *Mein Kampf* belonged in my uncle's Rotwelsch library, and not only because it was my grandfather's copy. It was a book whose purpose was to eliminate the world that had made Rotwelsch possible.

ROTWELSCH LESSON:
WAYS TO SAY POLICE IN ROTWELSCH

Blauer = (blue, also in combination with: blue helmet, blue collar, blue hat)

Bulle = (literally, a bull)

Deckel = (literally, a top, here used to refer to a helmet)

Diff

Fickler

Gansel = (Yiddish *gazlen*, rogue)

Greifer = (someone who grabs)

Hemann

Huscher = (someone who sneaks around)

Klisto

Lamfisel

Laterne = (lantern: someone who sheds light)

Mondschein = (moonlight)

Naderer = (secret police)

Polente = (possibly from Yiddish *palats*, for castle or palace)

Quetsch

Säbelhut = (saber-hat)

Schmiere = (guard, from *shmire*, to watch someone)

Spitzkopf = ("pointy head," based on the shape of a military helmet)

Chapter 5

THE KING OF THE TRAMPS

———

As I was trying to understand my uncle's work on Rotwelsch, and the motivation of its enemies for trying to eliminate it, I decided to go back to the origin of his literary activities: a journal he and my father had started while living in the commune during the 1960s.[1] Growing up, I would occasionally come across an old issue lying in a corner. My father published under his own name, while my uncle chose a pseudonym, Martin Groddeck, supposedly (according to my cousin) to make it look like there were more nonfamily contributors than was actually the case. The two brothers called themselves Günter and Herbert Puchner Publishers.

I particularly liked the graphic designer, Werner Beulecke, who gave the journal its distinctive look, crawling with starkly drawn absurdist figures with large heads and gangly, insectlike limbs. He also made a portrait of my father, capturing his round head, a lock of thinning hair combed across his forehead, a gen-

erous mustache, one hand holding a flask. The drawing is my favorite depiction of my father and now hangs above my desk.

The journal was the beginning of my uncle's literary career (and also my father's). But going through the journal, I couldn't find a single trace of Rotwelsch. At the time, Günter still thought of himself primarily as a composer, but as the sixties wore on, he turned more toward literature, until he discovered Rotwelsch and decided to commit himself to the language. I still wasn't sure what exactly had attracted him to it. Was it simply that this language would allow him to access the life of vagrants? Short of joining the itinerant underground, the language was as close as he was going to get to their world.

What about my father? He didn't turn his life over to poetry the way my uncle would do with Rotwelsch, but poetry asserted itself, mostly at moments of doubt, when he thought about the past and the future late at night, when he despaired and when he thought himself a failure. It hadn't started that way. In the journal, both brothers used literature as part of a generational rebellion, to assert their voices, to change German culture. They didn't have a clear plan, only a purpose and an attitude. But then, over time, this literary experiment changed, for both of them, turning into a lifelong occupation for one, and a lifelong nocturnal activity for the other. Was my uncle thinking of his brother as he pieced together his Rotwelsch archive, the outgrowth of their literary collaboration? And my father, was he thinking of his brother when he wrote his poems at night?

=

While the journal didn't tell me much about Rotwelsch, it led me to an intriguing figure: Gregor Gog. He, too, had started a journal, which was perhaps why he was everywhere in my uncle's archive.

Gog's mother had once promised God that her son would join the priesthood, and young Gregor duly served four long years as an altar boy. Then he had enough. He enlisted in the German merchant marine, got himself to East Asia, deserted, returned to Germany to work as a gardener, enlisted in World War I, became a traveling salesman, quit, traveled to Brazil, returned, and started to associate with various religiously inspired seekers and cultish groups that were springing up in southern Germany.[2]

Along the way, Gog hung out with drifters, misfits, bohemians, and tramps, of which there were more and more as economic convulsions rattled the young Weimar Republic. Gog also started to write about his experiences on the road. Above all, he developed a plan: tramps needed to organize. He started an international brotherhood of tramps and called for a meeting in southern Germany, in 1929. The timing was perfect. They came from everywhere, even though they were not welcome in the regional town of Stuttgart, which was very proper and bourgeois. But tramps weren't easily deterred. They knew how to make do, and they didn't need hotel reservations or train tickets.

Gregor Gog

All they needed was word of mouth and they came, over six hundred of them, because they knew that something had to be done.

Those who couldn't come sent greetings, including Sinclair Lewis, who regretted that he couldn't attend in person because he was tramping around the United States. Maksim Gorky, the celebrated Russian writer of *The Lower Depths*, a play set in a flophouse, approved of the undertaking and sent word that he wished he could be there.[3] One prominent figure who didn't join in was Charlie Chaplin, even though Gog looked a little bit like him, sporting his own mustache.

Chaplin had done something unusual: in *The Tramp*, the silent film he wrote and directed, released in 1915, he turned the tramp into a protagonist. The modern world with its borders and passports had treated travelers as criminals, but, for the first time, on screen one was becoming a hero: a small figure wearing a derby, a mustache, pants that were way too large, and carrying a cane. He had a way of walking somewhere between the gait of a dancer and a duck. Chaplin's tramp would become the perfect icon for the Great Depression, a time of mass unemployment, when people were thrown out of their houses and onto the road, and another wave of vagrancy was created, like the Thirty Years War and its aftermath.

While Chaplin had turned tramps into modern heroes, Gog proposed to organize them into a movement. By the time Gog's gathering of tramps happened, he had acquired a new name, or rather a title: King of the Tramps. It was half joke, half real. "To be a tramp, I don't need a boss," one dissident grumbled.[4] Others questioned whether Gog even was a real tramp, especially after it became known that he had built a cabin for himself. True, he was willing to put up anyone who came his way, but was that enough? Some called the establishment "villa Gregor

Gog."[5] Things got worse when a movie director, Fritz Weiss, chose him as a central character for a documentary film on vagrants. Gog cooperated and soon a camera team showed up at his "villa," eager to film how the King of the Tramps fulfilled his leadership responsibilities. Gog enjoyed the film, but it further damaged his reputation on the road.

Those who criticized Gog for his new fame had a point—who's ever heard of a tramp with a villa, starring in a movie?—but Gog had something better: a vision. What made someone a tramp? Was it the lack of a home, or was it a state of mind? Karl Marx had said that tramps had no real sense of themselves as a distinct group. They were the lumpen proletariat, the "ragged proletarians" from whom no class consciousness could be expected.[6]

Gog believed otherwise. He recognized that vagrants were different from everyone else, that they had been persecuted, their mode of life outlawed, that they had been arrested for having the wrong papers, or no papers, or simply for being who they were. To better their lot, tramps needed to band together, become self-aware vagrants, and demand change. A true vagabond wasn't just anyone without a home, but someone who embraced life on the road consciously and deliberately. Living at the rock bottom of society, wandering beggars were the ultimate critics of the modern world, the "saboteurs of the oppressive state."[7] Being on the road was an identity. Gog was not shy about exhibiting this identity and invited journalists to attend the gathering. Individual vagrants and families were ready to be photographed in this campaign to gain them recognition as a distinct group.

Seizing control of the narrative was also the point for Gog. I finally tracked down the film about him in a former SS facility

that now housed the National Archives in Berlin.[8] The film—a silent film, with Dutch intertitles—begins with the humiliating rituals of a tramp being abused by the police, sent to a homeless shelter, and ordered to strip to be deloused (there are about twenty different Rotwelsch words for lice). But mostly, the film revolves around Gog and his entourage assembled at his "villa." Most of them are men, but I noticed a few women among them, one of them Jo Mihaly.

While a teenager, Mihaly (her professional name; she was born Elfriede Alice Kuhr) wrote a diary about the experience of World War I and became a committed antiwar activist. She trained as a dancer, mostly performing in antiwar programs on small stages. During the Great Depression, she drifted into the itinerant underground and became a member of Gog's entourage, raising the consciousness of vagrants. I found footage of another documentary, from the 1980s, in which she spoke

about life on the road, and the identity of being a traveler, without romance but with great dignity.

Because the Gog film was silent, I couldn't hear the conversation among the itinerants, but the footage provided me with
a clue of how to get to know their thoughts after all: a journal
called *The Vagrant* (*Der Kunde*). The journal, to which Mihaly
contributed, served as a crucial prop in the film and was presented as the reason that Gog, who edited it, was so crucial to
the itinerant underground, its king.

The predecessor of today's street newspapers put together
and sold by homeless people, *The Vagrant* allowed tramps to
raise their own voice. For centuries, they had only been spoken about, and mostly negatively. Now, they could speak and
write for themselves. In *The Vagrant*, tramps didn't always
agree on what it meant to be a vagrant, but they shared an
experience of both hardship and freedom. No one who hadn't
experienced this combination could imagine how it felt to be
exposed to the elements for years on end, facing hunger, illness, solitude, the chicaneries of homeless shelters, the police,
and prison. There were many reasons tramps found themselves outside the established order, that they couldn't cope
with the requirements of modern, settled life. Being on the
road was an affliction.

But hardship was only one part of itinerant life. The other
part was liberty. Representatives of the settled world tended
to diagnose in vagrants a "pathological tendency to wander,"
and they weren't necessarily wrong.[9] Some vagrants developed
a taste for the road. The more their memories of settled life
faded, the more difficult it was for them to imagine a life without wandering. "There is a line that goes through my life: the
road," one of them wrote.[10] How could you imagine a life with-

out that line, without the very thing that was giving you direction and meaning?

As life on the road was becoming an identity, vagrants no longer thought of themselves as outcasts, as anomalies, as mentally ill. Living on the road, traveling, giving up on a fixed abode was what some of the boldest and most admired humans had done, including Christopher Columbus, Jesus, and Gandhi.[11] Wandering across the face of the earth was something many humans had been doing all along; it was the ultimate human condition.[12] One vagrant added, poetically, that even the stars wander across the sky, and he quoted the early Greek philosopher Heraclitus, who had said that everything was in motion and that standing still, settling down, and putting down roots, was an illusion.[13]

In Gog's journal, tramps defended not only their way of life but also their *kochemer loshn*. Some called themselves *kunden*, derived from *ken*, meaning right.[14] One tramp recounted a conversation by which a man and a woman test each other to find out whether they belong to the fellowship of the road.

> Man: Are you wiz (*Kunde*)?
> Woman: I'm Wiz Mathilde.
> Man: What's your religion?
> Woman: I've been eating cabbage.[15]

Translation:

> Man: Are you an initiate in the ways of the road?
> Woman: Yes, I'm an initiate. My name is Mathilde.
> Man: What's your profession?
> Woman: I've recently been in prison.

"Religion" in Rotwelsch means profession or role in the underground. If you answer "Lutheran" or "Catholic," you reveal yourself as an outsider. If you know how to shmooze in the *kochemer loshn*, you answer with something like: I'm a black artist, meaning chimney sweep, or that you're a professional fisherman—i.e., a thief.

The writers were proud of their language and knew its history. One tramp explained that it was after the Thirty Years War that Rotwelsch acquired many Hebrew terms because Jews were chased from one jurisdiction to the next and were forced to mingle with other vagrants.[16] Yes, these vagrants admitted, to some extent Rotwelsch was a secretive language, but for the most part, the purpose of shmoozing in this language was not to hatch plots. Rather, Rotwelsch was their authentic way of talking, which had developed alongside other itinerant languages such as Yiddish and Romani, and an expression of their distinct way of life. It was simply how they spoke.

This was a completely new tone and voice. Since Luther, Rotwelsch had been written down only by its enemies, by people who wanted to decode the language or eliminate it or, on rare occasions, study it. But now, vagrants were writing about Rotwelsch themselves, offering a completely new perspective on it. I even began to wonder whether the few reports of parents forcing their children to speak Rotwelsch, or of gangs deliberately adding words and spreading them, were to be trusted. Wasn't all this a paranoid fantasy on the part of the police, of the forces of law and order, of writers warning upright citizens again and again, for centuries, about the secret doings of the underground? Similar fantasies were captured in such works as John Gay's *Beggar's Opera* (1728) and its modern adaptation, Bertolt Brecht's *Threepenny Opera* (1928), both of which depict an underground that was every bit as organized as the official world, with its own king, institutions, and language.

Gangs getting together and agreeing on secret words—this was not how languages actually emerged. Rotwelsch developed among outcasts in response to their shared life experiences. These included constant feelings of vulnerability, of being exposed to the weather, hunger, illness, and the threat of being arrested. We sometimes refer to communication intended for a milieu or profession as "jargon," a pejorative term for someone else's incomprehensible way of speaking. But what, for an outsider, sounds like jargon is for an insider a convenient and efficient expression of a group's mode of life, a sociolect. If the group is hunted by the police, then there will be many expressions for "police." If the group consists of horse traders (who developed a distinct language that overlapped with Rotwelsch), there will be many technical terms relating to the value of horses. Communication works best when it can rely on shared assumptions and expertise. If you have to spell everything out, communication channels get clogged.

The problem is that the same thing that speeds up communication within a group—namely, in-group shortcuts—also makes it difficult for outsiders to understand. But this doesn't mean that secrecy is the main purpose of such a language. I started to wonder whether the entire idea that Rotwelsch was a secret language was something of a projection, as had also been the case of Yiddish, produced by its enemies. Both were languages spoken by distinct subgroups, expressing each group's life and serving to create community. In both cases, the charge of secrecy was connected to anti-Semitism.

Jargon is especially important for marginal groups or other communities living outside the mainstream. They need to cultivate shared experiences and expertise to defend themselves against more powerful majorities. What Gog, Mihaly—and my uncle—were celebrating was essentially a cultural right to jargon.

When Hitler assumed power in 1933, this right ceased to exist. Vagrants were labeled "asocial" and were among the first to be picked up by the Gestapo, the newly empowered secret state police, and the SA (Sturmabteilung, or Storm Troopers), Hitler's own paramilitary group. Jo Mihaly fled to Zurich, but Gregor Gog was arrested, and all materials connected with *The Vagrant* were confiscated.[17] Gog spent time in Nazi Germany's earliest concentration camps, such as KZ Heuberg, KZ Reutlingen, and KZ Ulm. Undesirables such as Gog didn't need to be convicted of a crime. They were simply taken into "protective custody," not to protect them, but to protect Germany from them.

Fortunately, Gog escaped to Switzerland—some said by crossing the frozen Lake Constance; others, through the help of a heavily pregnant woman, who distracted the border guards and let him pass as her husband.[18] From Switzerland, he made it to Moscow, in 1934. Looking back at his experience, he reported on his time in concentration camps and the vagrants he met there, fellow tramps as young as seventeen and as old as seventy, all victims of what Gog called "Goebbels's hunt for vagrants."[19] Being hunted by "fascist barbarians," Gog said, made him escape from Hitler's Germany and seek refuge in the workers' republic, where he had been once before.

But Hitler's Germany wasn't done hunting him. In June 1941, Hitler broke the secret pact with the Soviet Union and attacked. Stalin was warned of this but didn't believe his advisors, leaving the USSR unprepared for the German onslaught.

Gog, along with many others, fled farther east, to Fergana, in Uzbekistan. Having become a Soviet citizen, he was drafted to do forced labor in Kazakhstan, then released and sent back to Uzbekistan, where he began work on a novel about the Battle of Stalingrad. He died of a kidney illness, before he could finish his work, on October 7, 1945.[20]

Without its journal—and its king—Rotwelsch barely survived the systematic incarceration and elimination of vagrants by the Nazi regime. The experience of the camps left its mark on the language, which acquired a new word: *kapo*, a prisoner assigned to supervise forced labor in concentration camps.

Jo Mihaly survived the war and spent the rest of her life championing her causes in Switzerland and beyond. Her World War I diary was published and eventually translated into English; she wrote about her experience in various ways and lived, as Grinder Berbel probably did, well into her eighties.

═══

Gog's journal was the first place where I encountered Rotwelsch speakers writing about their own language. I began hunting for other occasions when they, not the police, produced a written record of their way of talking. And I hit the jackpot. Guided by my uncle's archive, I tracked down, in the basement of Jena city hall, a unique source dealing with the case of a vagrant called Ferdinand Baumhauer.[21] I hadn't spent a lot of time in East Germany, which seemed stuck in time. I was staying at an inn that had once been frequented by Martin Luther. A friendly archivist, who usually dealt with property disputes, handed me the two volumes and directed me to a separate room, with none of the security measures usually employed by more professional archives.

I sat in front of the two thick binders, slightly awed. The Baumhauer source is an anomaly, the only time that an actual Rotwelsch speaker wrote not only *about* Rotwelsch but *in* Rotwelsch.

Born in 1818 into a family of cotton weavers, Baumhauer had apprenticed himself to a cobbler at age thirteen, completed the apprenticeship a few years later, and begun the customary years as a journeyman, hoping to learn from other masters of the trade. He found work with another master, and little seemed to stand in the way of his pursuing a career as a skilled artisan. But things didn't work out that way. Baumhauer quarreled with a fellow apprentice and abruptly left his position. Seeking cheap accommodation for the night, he chanced upon a shelter favored by tramps, his first contact with the people of the road. Something about them must have appealed to him, or perhaps he was tired of having to serve masters who were often strict and abusive. He decided to quit his life as a journeyman and begin a much more precarious life as a vagrant.

Journeymen carried papers that allowed them to travel freely, following the practice recommended by Martin Luther, but Baumhauer was no longer one of them. Local authorities would stop anyone who looked like a vagrant and didn't have proper documentation.

Yet, as registries and the requirement of carrying papers had spread since Luther's time, so too had the demand for forgery. Baumhauer's first attempt at forging papers was pitiful and led to a short prison sentence, but soon he got better at it and even started to help out fellow vagrants with his newly developed skill. Baumhauer now contributed his part to the solidarity among tramps and hoboes by fabricating stamps and seals, imitating signatures and doctoring papers. He had found his niche in the ecosystem of the road, which, like other Rotwelsch speakers, he divided into different land districts called *martine* (from the Yiddish *medine*, for land).

After being *on martine* (on the road) around Bohemia, which was relatively tolerant toward itinerants, he crossed into Germany (called *Aschkunesische Martine* in Rotwelsch) and was apprehended by the Jena police in 1843, at the age of twenty-five. His police file describes him as stocky, dressed in a black coat, with blond hair, an oval face, a large, crooked as well as pointy nose, and bad teeth. His religion is identified as Lutheran.

His papers were revealed to be forgeries, and Baumhauer was made to confess; the source doesn't mention the methods by which this confession was extracted. Baumhauer eventually provided the names and locations of dozens of associates and their preferred hangouts. The Jena police—above all, Police Inspector Flemming—were mightily pleased with their catch.

Flemming was even more pleased when he realized that Baumhauer had an unusual skill for a vagrant: he was a good scribe, what Rotwelsch speakers would call a *sofer* (from Yiddish and Hebrew), thanks to years of forging papers. Flemming asked his prisoner to write down scenes from life in the underground. Baumhauer complied, filling a book with scenes of vagrancy in Rotwelsch. Baumhauer was a perfect informant, a Rotwelsch speaker with good penmanship. He even provided the decryption key—the meanings of secret words—on the right-hand side of each page and added helpful information at the bottom in the form of footnotes, aware of how little the police would know about the life he was describing.

Baumhauer used the old-fashioned German script, or *Kurrent*. It took me days to decipher it, but once I did, his scenes opened up the experience of life on the road. Baumhauer's main characters are Walter and his female companion, Walteress. They travel with a wagon, a horse, and several children from village to village, by begging, thieving, and peddling small goods. It was illegal in one way or another because they didn't have the necessary permits for crossing these lands, the kind of permission granted to a pilgrim or official merchant, which meant that any encounter with the police could lead to arrest. Baumhauer describes several such encounters in which his protagonists barely get away, as well as scenes in which Rotwelsch speakers trick simple farmers or band together in large gangs.

In these scenes—plays, really, complete with stage directions, even though not written to be performed—Baumhauer reveals what no police examination could have uncovered, namely, how Rotwelsch was actually used. In this way, he became the most authentic source for the jargon of the underworld. In his account, the people of the road often switch between Rotwelsch and various dialects, speaking Rotwelsch among themselves, but also when they don't want to be understood by others. This confirmed that there was something secretive about Rotwelsch, but not how this secrecy had emerged. Certainly, Baumhauer didn't describe scenes in which the underworld took standard German or Yiddish terms and made them incomprehensible. In any case, Baumhauer was writing under duress: nothing he wrote could be taken at face value.

Did Flemming have Baumhauer read these strange plays out loud to show how Rotwelsch words were pronounced? Or was the police inspector so pleased with Baumhauer's creation that he organized readings of this Rotwelsch play for his own amusement? It is hard to imagine. Most likely, the transaction was more mundane: the police wanted a piece of text to decipher the language, and Baumhauer complied to get in good with his jailers.

It was from Baumhauer that my uncle must have learned many of the expressions I liked best, such as *sweetling* for sugar and *roundling* for potato, as well as inventive words for police (*polente*, perhaps from the Yiddish *palats* for palace) and prison (*palais*, palace in French, or *schul*, for school). Baumhauer also revealed many other words that dominated the lived reality of Rotwelsch speakers, with dozens of words for food, drink, sex (*chammelschiggis*, "a prostitute"), and lice (*chinnum*). Equally, there were many words for stealing and begging (to *mauschel*; to *rat*). In fact, stealing and begging, as done by Walteress in the village, were described by the same word, as were stolen and traded goods (from the Yiddish *skhoyre*): *sore*.

One of the scenes written down by Baumhauer is of Walter and Walteress making a narrow escape. A mounted policeman stops Walter to check their papers (undoubtedly forged) while Walteress has gone to get her hands on some *sore* in a nearby village. Walter convinces the policeman that nothing untoward is happening, but then the policeman hears dogs barking in the village and senses that something isn't right. Walter has already left by this time, and Walteress, thinking quickly on her feet, avoids the policeman and meets up with Walter farther away. By now the policeman realizes that he has been fooled and pursues them. Fortunately, the Walter wagon races ahead and crosses the border to the next jurisdiction.

I have no doubt that Baumhauer took this scene from life; he knew all about escape. Once he had finished his Rotwelsch stories, the police relaxed their vigilance and Baumhauer fled. His confession and his writing had served him as a ruse, a distraction that allowed him to get away. No doubt he was familiar with my favorite Rotwelsch expression, *an hasn machn*, for making a rabbit. It's the most essential thing about life on the road: whether you're chased by the police or not, whether you're carrying forged papers or not, you're always escaping, even if you don't have a particular destination in mind.

=

Making a rabbit is deeply written into the mythology of my family. A nineteenth-century ancestor, discovered by my grandfather, had been a schoolteacher, with a wife and children. One day, this man left his family and his job behind, taking nothing with him but his violin. For the rest of his life, he worked as a traveling musician, playing at weddings and other occasions, leading an itinerant life on the road. Perhaps he was even inducted into Rotwelsch.

The name of this wandering musician was Hans Martin Puchner, and I am named after him. My father told me this shortly after he bought me my first violin, and whenever I play now, I think of my father and my namesake. In my family, playing violin is part of the idea of making a rabbit. My father often described to me that as a young man, he would go into the forest and play there for hours. When I was in college, a friend and I planned to spend the summer traveling around Italy, making ends meet as street musicians. The plan was flawed because my friend didn't play any instrument; and we both chickened out at the last minute and stayed home. But the idea was there.

When he wasn't writing poetry about failure and violins, had my father been brooding over making a rabbit himself, perhaps with his own violin in hand? Had he named me Hans Martin Puchner because leaving was what he wanted to do himself?

In the last years of his life, my father would go out pretty much every evening and go to the dive bar around the corner, where he was known as the Professor. It was true, of course: he was a professor, a professor of architecture at the local technical college, a job he enjoyed as much as running his small architectural practice. I would sometimes sit in on his lectures, especially those on the principles of design. My father was enamored of the golden mean, a beautiful mathematical principle, used by Leonardo da Vinci, which can also be found in the nautilus, a mollusk with a perfectly regular spiral shell.

This widely liked professor of architecture went regularly around the corner to become the Professor among the local drunks. He also had affairs, as I learned once I left for college and my mother complained about them in late-night phone calls. An Australian exchange student I remembered, who suddenly had shown up at our house, was one of them. I was forced to reconsider the story of my family, assimilating the new information. It was odd: it was only when I moved out that I began to learn the truth about the household I'd grown up in. Perhaps I hadn't wanted to ask too many questions, happy to hold on to an illusion of harmony. Confused and angry, I finally asked my mother to stop calling me. I didn't want to know more details.

I know that my father loved his family. I know it in every fiber of my body, in every memory of him; I know it because of his unfailing generosity, his commitment to our welfare, his open, gregarious temperament, and his unselfish nature. He loved my mother deeply, and she, him. During the last ten years of his life, they found a quiet way of conducting their marriage, supporting their three children with selfless dedication.

But I also know—and deep in my heart I have always known—that he harbored the fantasy of running away, that there were times when he felt outsmarted by life. His hopes and yearnings were unfulfilled, and he saw himself a failure. The dive bar, the affairs, the alcohol, were all strategies of avoidance. Being in a pickle and making a rabbit: these two Rotwelsch expressions pretty much sum up his life.

The most precious of my father's possessions that I inherited, besides his violin, is his flask, which also features in the Beulecke portrait of him. He once told me he loved the design, a simple modernist form that was slightly curved to fit the shape of the human chest, with a neat mechanism for holding the screw-on cap in place. A great invention, the flask. It allows you to have a drink while you're on the road.

ROTWELSCH LESSON:
GETTING AWAY IN ROTWELSCH

Absent geben = to go absent
An hasn machn = to make a rabbit
Auf Martine gehen (to go on *martine*) = to cross the land
Kraut fressen = to eat weed
Naschen = to snack
Quetschen
Schiebes machen = to make an escape
Schiebes naschen
Schwellen

Stromen = to be on the street, from *Strom*, for bordello
Tippeln
Trollen
Wandern = to wander about

Individual Zinken *and Warnings*[22]

A warning of betrayal (cock means betrayal, a biblical reference).

Symbol of a professional card shark.

Zinken for a female vagrant who steals while the shopkeeper measures and cuts wares for other customers.

Zinken of a woman open to sexual contact (bared breasts).

Chapter 6

THE FARMER AND THE JUDGE

———

"My grandfather was sent to a concentration camp." This was pretty much the first thing my mother would say to my American girlfriends, including my partner Amanda, who came to Nuremberg shortly after my father's death. The statement was Amanda's introduction to my family.

I knew the outlines of my mother's story, but the sentence about the concentration camp came back to me now, while I was digesting the discoveries about my paternal grandfather and wondering about his children. It was never easy to talk to my mother about the past. I had tried to draw her out about life in the commune, but she had little good to say about it. She had grown up on a remote farm in southern Germany, in difficult circumstances. Forced to leave school at fourteen to apprentice herself to a seamstress, she persuaded the village priest to teach her Latin and arrange for her to go to a Catholic boarding school attached to a convent. She was the first person in her village to do so.

When, after convent school, my mother found herself in the worldly city of Munich, with its grand streets, palaces, and government buildings, she was overawed. What she hadn't expected was that she would find herself living with a bunch of bohemians: this was not what moving from a farm to the city was supposed to look like.

Later, whenever the topic of the commune came up, she would complain about the three men who would disappear into a room, making strange noises (the equivalent idiom in Rotwelsch literally means "going into the soup together"). "And no one was doing the dishes," she would add, outraged after all these years (there is no Rotwelsch expression for doing the dishes). On Sundays, instead of going to church, my father and his brother would go to the city's museums, where they made a habit of mooning the art. My mother, having grown up without access to museums, didn't have a lot of patience for this sort of rebellion.

The three men, the dishes, the mooning, and Rotwelsch were prime examples of things that were "not very nice," which my mother pronounced as one word. She didn't like talking about this notverynice period. When I managed to persuade her, she would speak in clipped sentences, her lips pressed together in disapproval. I am amazed that she stuck it out for as long as she did, living in that apartment under those circumstances. She must have approached it with the same dogged determination as the convent school and university. When my father finally finished his degree and got a job—she was already working as a village school teacher—she was delighted to move out.

Now that I had developed an interest in the family's history, she was even more careful, worried about saying the wrong thing. Since my new interest had first emerged a few years after I had moved to America, I sensed there was something else at stake. Even though she hadn't said much, I knew that it was hard for her that I had moved to America, and it was becoming increasingly clear that I wasn't coming back any time soon. After my father's death, my living abroad was particularly difficult for her (for me as well). She now developed another idea: "Martin, you are the head of the family." It was immensely meaningful to her, this phrase, and she kept repeating it. At the time, I would simply answer: "Why me? My brothers can do it." I was the oldest, true, but I was living far away, while one brother, Stephan, not even two years younger, was living an hour's train ride from Nuremberg. (My younger brother, a teenager at the time, would later move to America as well.)

It's a strange thing about family folkways that only now, as I am writing these lines, does it occur to me how strange the phrase "head of the family" really is. It sounded like we were a mafia outfit in which the oldest son naturally became *capo* after the father's death, otherwise rival families would take over our territories. Perhaps my mother used the phrase unconsciously to lure me back home. Nothing I did or said could dislodge her insistence.

If my mother had become more careful about the past, especially now that I began asking questions, she was more forthcoming about her own childhood. She described to me, in more detail than usual, how she had grown up on a farm whose owners were hostile to her because she'd been born out of wedlock. Her father, the oldest son of the farmer, was cajoled into marrying my grandmother when the second child was on its way. There is no good German (or Rotwelsch) word for shotgun wedding, but that's what it was. In accordance with custom in cases where the bride was no longer a virgin, my grandmother wore a black wedding gown.

It was in the middle of World War II, and my mother saw her father only when he was home during rare leave from the front. The family received occasional mail, in which this provincial farmer gave them news of the larger world into which the war had thrust him. In Strasbourg, on the border with France, he attended his first opera performance and saw his first movie. Then he was moved to the eastern front and found himself in Ukraine. When he wrote home for swimming trunks, which he intended to use in the Black Sea, there was grumbling that he was having too much fun. He wrote back that he could hear the detonations from the front, twenty miles away.

Things got worse for him after parts of the German army (not his battalion) were encircled and decimated at Stalingrad, the turning point on the eastern front, when the seemingly invincible Wehrmacht was stopped and, ultimately, forced to retreat. My grandfather was driven back step by step, first through Ukraine and then Poland. There was no more swimming, or opera. In January 1945, he was driving a truck with wounded soldiers south of Kraków when a shell hit the car in front of him. Most of his comrades died in the ensuing battle and the family received no more news; along with so many others, he was missing in action.

The war ended, southern Germany was occupied by the American army, and the situation was still difficult for the family, which now consisted of my grandmother, my mother, and her two siblings (the youngest, a son, had been born in the meanwhile). They were living on a farm against the wishes of the farm's owners because of the shotgun wedding. Now that the firstborn son was missing, other members of the family were hoping to take over the farm.

In 1949, a former army comrade, who had been in Russian captivity, wrote to give the family certain news that their son had died in the battle four years earlier. He had stepped out of his truck and been struck by a bullet almost immediately. Now that his death was confirmed, things became even more difficult for my mother's family. The farmer's second son, Xaver, tried to bully them into giving up their claim on the farm, and when that didn't work, he tried to strangle my grandmother. She ran to her father's farm, but her father persuaded her to hold her ground and returned her with the local policeman in tow. Finally a compromise was found and my grandmother and her three children moved to a nearby village.

===

While my mother was enduring the war years on the hostile farm, she spent as much time as possible on a much friendlier farm, the one run by Joseph Kresser, her paternal grandfather, an outspoken but, in her words, benevolent patriarch. As the war continued, he started listening to Allied radio and was overheard by a jealous neighbor saying that the American army would liberate them soon. The neighbor promptly reported him to the secret police. (Sometimes it was better to speak in code, as all Rotwelsch speakers know, but this was not the Rotwelsch side of my family.)

My great-grandfather was arrested, and other charges materialized. He was ultimately brought to Berlin and tried by the notorious Nazi judge Roland Freisler. Freisler had attended the Wannsee Conference where the "final solution to the Jewish problem" was decided, and he was one of the masterminds behind the Nuremberg Laws, which defined Jews as second-class citizens (and which dovetailed with my paternal grand-father's recommendations regarding Jewish names). Mostly, Freisler was known for running the most ideological court in the country, the so-called People's Court.[1] He was quick-witted, not a quality that was common among Nazis, and had a feeling for courtroom drama. He would humiliate prisoners and subject them to long, shouted harangues. Frequently, Freisler ordered guards to remove the belts of the accused, forcing them to hold up their pants with their hands. The People's Court was a theater as much as a court, a place where the Nazi perversion of the law was on full display, mixing childish pranks with bloodlust. Freisler was the personification of Nazi law and usually delivered death sentences, over five thousand of them.[2]

The family panicked. Friends suggested that at least two daughters should attend the trial and plead for their father's life if they wanted him to have any chance of survival. But how could they get to Berlin, which was hundreds of miles away? Where could they stay? And who could take them there, since the remaining adults were needed on the farm?

In their desperation, they came up with the plan of having the daughters chaperoned by the very neighbor who had denounced their father and who was taking the same train to testify against him. I found this hard to believe and asked my mother several times, and later an aunt, but that's how they all told the story. The trial was the typical ritual of humiliation. My great-grandfather, who had been in prison for over a year by then, had his belt taken away while Freisler ordered him to stand at attention, so that his pants fell to the floor.

Surprisingly, the family's desperate plan of sending two

daughters to plead for leniency worked. Freisler cross-examined witnesses, but for some reason he didn't seem as worried about the defeatism charge, of which my great-grandfather had already been convicted by a lower court. Freisler was worried about farmers. It was November 30, 1944, provisions were running low, which was why Freisler was worried about food supply. "Is he a good farmer?" he hollered. "Is his family helping out on the farm?" The witnesses, surprised, mumbled something in the affirmative. To everyone's astonishment, Freisler let the relatively lenient verdict of the lower court, which had decided on three years of penitentiary rather than the death penalty, stand. After subjecting my great-grandfather and others to long, shouted rants, Freisler didn't send him to the firing squad. Instead Freisler sent him to Sachsenhausen.

I base this account on the memories of Josefine Merk, my great-aunt and one of the daughters who attended the trial. Josefine dictated it in 2012, at the advanced age of ninety-six. She was lucid, possessed of a clear memory, and wanted this historic episode to be written down.

Sachsenhausen was one of the first concentration camps in Germany, located on the outskirts of Berlin and used to train the SS in the art of running concentration camps with maximum brutality. Initially it wasn't a death camp, but by the time my grandfather was tried and convicted in 1944, it had been retrofitted with gas chambers and ovens. Horrendous medical experiments, starvation, forced labor, and random killings took place there.[3]

Upon entering, Joseph Kresser would have been given the red badge that marked a political prisoner.[4] Jews wore yellow badges and Roma, brown. That's where my imagination stopped and I decided to visit the camp. Most of the buildings had been razed and all that remained was the imprint of their walls, displaying their symmetrical arrangement. The layout felt cold and calculating, geometry put in the service of terror. A few buildings were still standing, and I could go in. The thing that knocked the breath out of me was a large stone trough in the kitchen. Its official use was for washing potatoes. But I learned that occasionally, an SS man would use it to drown an inmate, just to show that he could. This was the true evil of the camp: even everyday objects—a shower, a trough—could suddenly become an instrument of torture. Nothing was left in life that was not tainted by death.

The best guide to the language of the camps is Primo Levi, who had been interned in Auschwitz together with a group of fellow deportees from Italy. In his book *If This Is a Man*, he describes the utter confusion of languages in the camps with cool detachment, which made the horror of what he was describing come alive all the more powerfully. After passing through the gate, prisoners were subject to hollered commands in German and needed to obey immediately. Primo Levi had studied chemistry, a field that at the time was dominated by German scientists, which meant that he had already picked up some German. "Knowing German meant life," he wrote.[5] Most of his fellow arrivals weren't so lucky. Survival became a question of language: "Most of the prisoners who did not know German—almost all the Italians, in other words—died within the first ten to fifteen days of their arrival."[6]

Levi also realized that the German of the camps was a strange, distorted version of the language as he knew it. The SS referred to eating as "feeding," speaking of inmates as if they were animals. The worst horrors were hidden behind a technical, bureaucratic lingo that inmates needed to decode. German-speaking inmates were at an advantage, though some German-speaking inmates reported that in addition to the devastation wrought on their bodies, they also had to endure the devastation wrought on their language. Because of the importance of German, the second most useful language in the camps was Yiddish because Yiddish speakers were able to understand their Nazi jailers better than, for example, Levi's fellow Italians.

Besides German and the Nazi-inflected version of it, a third language was spoken in the camps, or rather a mixture of languages. The SS left most of the day-to-day control of the inmates—from the distribution of food to the organization of work gangs—to other inmates, and these inmate-supervisors spoke a variety of languages, from Polish, Russian, Romanian, Czech, and Hungarian to Greek, French, and Italian. The word for "selection," the euphemism for deciding who would be sent to the gas chamber, was *selekcja*, a hybrid Latin-Hungarian word. Not understanding your foreman (*kapo*) was almost as dangerous as not understanding an SS soldier, leading at the very least to savage beatings. Physical violence, Levi writes, "was an evident part of their duties, their more or less accepted language, and, for that matter, the only language in that perpetual tower of Babel which could truly be understood by everyone."[7]

The Tower of Babel was Primo Levi's metaphor for language in the camps. Speakers of almost all European languages were forced together, misunderstanding one another. "The confusion of languages is a fundamental component of the way of life here."[8] Years after he had been freed, Levi would try out words and phrases he had learned in the camps, and have friends translate them for him. (This Babel-like chaos was also one reason, Levi noted, that organized resistance was almost impossible.)

As a German speaker and political prisoner, my great-grandfather would have belonged to a privileged group of concentration camp inmates. He may have been allowed to receive some mail; he would not have been subjected to the worst of the random violence that was inflicted on those deemed as subhuman by the SS.

In my research, I found a small booklet from Sachsenhausen containing camp songs. It could fit into the palm of a hand and was easy to hide.[9] The ornamentation suggested that originally it might have been intended as a notebook for girls.

The most popular song at Sachsenhausen was called "The Peat Bog Soldiers" (Moorsoldaten). The inmates imagine themselves to be soldiers who are marching to work in the morning and returning in the evening to their heavily guarded camp.

> We sleep behind barbed wire
> with sore and bleeding hands.
> We labor hard and toughen up
> But work just never ends.

The song, which goes through many strophes, ends on a note of desperate hope:

> There'll come a time when we will leave behind
> our coats with triangles and numbers
> and make our escape from misery and grief.
> Then we'll depart from Sachsenhausen,
> with the promise of freedom
> and the songs from home.
> Sing, comrades, sing!

The song had originated in another camp whose inmates were doing hard labor in a nearby moor, but had mysteriously spread to other camps, including Sachsenhausen. It was sung not only by inmates but also by their SS guards. Was the SS using it cynically, to keep their inmates' spirits up? For me it was something else, an expression on the part of the inmates of a desperate will to live even in the most inhuman of situations. The song was later recorded by Hanns Eisler, a collaborator of Bertolt Brecht, and I first heard it in that arrangement. (Paul Robeson recorded it in the early forties.) It has a catchy tune. One morning, soon after I first encountered it, I was humming it to myself without quite realizing, when Amanda asked me what it was. Only then did I grasp that I was singing a tune from Sachsenhausen over my morning coffee. It stopped me in my tracks, and I realized that for some time I had been imagining Joseph Kresser singing it, desperately holding on to the hope that he might be released.

While the song promised ultimate release, in reality more than thirty thousand inmates died at Sachsenhausen and many more were sent to death camps. But Joseph Kresser was not among them; for him the song's promise held true. Josefine, his daughter, writes that when the Russian army was approaching, the SS marched prisoners into the woods and left them there. Afraid that they would be shot, the prisoners remained standing for a long time until they realized that their tormentors were gone.

Josefine remembered the day, in August 1945, when a vagrant showed up at the farm. At first no one knew what to do with him. Then the vagrant identified himself as Joseph Kresser, her father. He had walked back through war-torn Germany for several months, under the cover of night. It would take him many more months to get his bearings and to return to a semblance of his old life. After his arrival, he kept to a dark room for weeks. My mother said that his eyes needed to adjust to light gradually, but I think there is more to the story. Remaining in your room for weeks, unable to come out: this sounds like serious trauma, unsurprising given what he must have witnessed in the camp, perhaps coupled with guilt at survival, of which so many survivors speak. This once proud farmer returned from Sachsenhausen a broken man. During the war and in prison he had talked too much; now he talked very little.

=====

The more I read about Sachsenhausen, the more the story of Joseph Kresser struck me as remarkable, almost unbelievable. Why had the notorious Nazi judge Freisler bothered to have my great-grandfather, this simple if irascible farmer, transported to Berlin at a time when Allied armies were closing in on Germany? Didn't the Nazis have better things to do? And how had my great-grandfather ended up in a concentration camp? Finally, how had he made it out of Sachsenhausen so relatively easily, when thousands were put on death marches or shot or left behind to die?

I began looking for documents to supplement the family stories. One box of documents came from Josefine's daughter. Various archives provided additional materials that gave me clues about the trial, the charges, and how my great-grandfather had been punished. The story that emerged from these documents confirmed important parts of the orally transmitted family stories, but not all of them.

It was true that my great-grandfather had been denounced by a neighbor for remarking, after the fall of Hitler's ally Mussolini, that he hoped the Americans would restore freedom in Germany. As a consequence, he had been tried for defeatism in Stuttgart, in southern Germany, convicted, and sentenced to three years of imprisonment and "loss of honor," which meant that he would no longer be in charge of his farm. He was sent to a nearby prison. He kept talking his mouth off even in prison, speaking against Hitler. He was denounced again and brought to Berlin to be tried by Roland Freisler as a recalcitrant defeatist who needed to be dealt with by the People's Court. While awaiting trial, he was taken to the notorious prison Moabit. (Rotwelsch speakers had long known this particular prison, which still exists, as *mockum*, the Yiddish word for place. For vagrants, being taken to the "town" of Berlin and being taken to Moabit prison was the same thing.[10]) I found internal documents in which the prosecutor declared that he would probably be seeking the death penalty.[11] But during the trial, the witnesses from the prison withdrew their testimony. Freisler declared contemptuously that "anyone could tell that he [Kresser] was of very limited mental capacities," but also a hardworking farmer.[12] He let the lower court's verdict stand.

At this point, the stories diverge. Prisoners convicted by the courts, even by Freisler's People's Court, almost never ended up in concentration camps, I learned, at least not directly. Either they were sentenced to death and executed, or they served their sentences in penitentiaries and prisons (it was only after serving their sentence that political prisoners like my great-grandfather might be taken to concentration camps under the doctrine of "protective custody"). I located a document that indicated that my great-grandfather had served several months of his sentence, until the end of the war, in Coswig, south of Berlin, not in Sachsenhausen.[13]

Coswig was no luxury hotel. It was what Rotwelsch speakers called a particularly vicious "school." I went to Coswig, located an hour and a half outside Berlin, to get an impression of the place. The train dropped me at a small village in the middle of nowhere, on the side of the rail tracks, from where I was to get a connection to Coswig. The derelict train station was abandoned and up for sale. After an hour of waiting for the next train, I used a phone booth to call for information. An annoyed voice informed me that it wasn't worth making regular stops in this small village anymore and that travelers transferring to Coswig should call to schedule a pickup. After another hour, a minibus came and grudgingly took me to my destination.

Located on the beautiful river Elbe, Coswig today is dominated by closed shopfronts and campaign posters for Alternative for Germany, the new right-wing party (known by its German initials, AfD). I walked through town until I saw the building that had served as the penitentiary. It didn't look like a prison at all, more like an elegant castle, built right on the river. That's what it had originally been—a castle—and it had been turned into a prison only in the nineteenth century, after its last owner had died. Now it was abandoned. I climbed into the moat, which was overgrown with poison ivy, but I couldn't get into the main building. When I looked at it from the distance, I saw that the old clock in the clock tower was still working. Was there someone lurking inside, winding it up from time to time?

The prison conditions had initially been harsh, but over the course of the nineteenth century various prison reforms had taken place, in keeping with more modern approaches to policing and punishment. After the Nazis came to power, they reconfigured the building to make the lives of convicts "extremely unpleasant,"[14] even though they left in place vestiges of more lenient times, including a now neglected prison library. The Nazis distinguished between different types of prisoners, with those in the higher rungs being allowed certain privileges, such as decorating their cells, keeping their light on until 9:00 p.m., and procuring additional food. Unfortunately for my great-grandfather, political prisoners were excluded from this system of privileges.

Prisoners were forced to do hard labor. They were marched through town handcuffed to one another on their way to nearby factories, including a soda factory and various weapons factories. They were also used as agricultural laborers as well as for a large-scale project designed to regulate the flow of the river Elbe, deepening the riverbed. Coswig inmates later reported extremely crowded conditions and lice infestations at the prison, and those working on the river were housed in unheated factories. When not on loan, political prisoners such as my great-grandfather were stuck in the attic of the penitentiary, in primitive conditions.[15]

Despite these harsh circumstances, there were no deaths reported at Coswig until 1941, when the bad air in the damp cells led to several outbreaks of tuberculosis. Between 1941 and 1944, 259 prisoners died, and in the first months of 1945, the time Joseph Kresser spent there, the death toll rose steeply, to 136 in four months. But there were no executions except on two occasions. After the assassination attempt on Hitler on July 20, 1944, the SS shot a group of inmates accused of being collaborators. On April 12, 1945, the Gestapo executed seven inmates accused of being sex offenders, which was a code word for homosexuality.

All of this must have been frightening, but Coswig was a far cry from Sachsenhausen. The purpose of Coswig was to punish prisoners by extracting labor from them, not "death-through-labor," as was the policy of the concentration camp system. There were no ovens. Had Joseph Kresser been convicted a few years earlier, he might have ended up in Sachsenhausen after completing his prison sentence, but he didn't, because the war was over before he could be sent there.

The liberation of Coswig was very different from that of Sachsenhausen. Sachsenhausen prisoners were not, as the family story had it, marched into the woods and left to escape on their own. They were taken north on notorious death marches, with those too weak to walk shot and left behind. Thousands died.

The end of Coswig was much less brutal. On April 27, the Russian 58th Guards Division, led by Major General Vladimir Rusakov, and the U.S. 69th Infantry Division, commanded by Major General Emil F. Reinhardt, converged on the river Elbe thirty-seven miles south of Cowsig. The two generals shook hands, a historic moment of the two great Allied armies meeting in the middle of Germany.

A few days later, on May 2, the two armies entered Coswig, meeting again on Wittenberger Strasse. According to the Yalta agreement, the Russian army was to be in possession of the city, and Major General Reinhardt complied with the treaty, taking the 69th Division back west. The Russians took control of the penitentiary and began looking for perpetrators of Nazi injustice. The prison doctor preempted them by killing himself with poison. There were trials against prison guards and against the commandant, Dr. Kluge, who was accused of having plotted to poison prisoners when the Russian army approached. Perhaps my great-grandfather had been in greater danger than I had realized. The trial ended without a conviction, and Dr. Kluge was rehabilitated.

Some official at Coswig decided to release most of the prisoners before the arrival of the Russian army. Josefine had preserved a barely legible fragment of a document stating that the prisoner Joseph Kresser was let go on April 27, 1945.

Having such a document in your possession was crucial. If the SS encountered a man without papers, he would be shot for desertion. The release document also states that my great-grandfather was given one hundred *marks* and food rations for two days, a far cry from the death marches of Sachsenhausen. This piece of paper was a lifesaver for Joseph Kresser.

===

The next time I saw my mother—she was visiting me in Cambridge—I told her what I had found out. It was summer, we had just spent some time on the shore, and were both tired.

"Do you remember Joseph ever talking about Sachsenhausen?"
"Yes, of course, he went to the concentration camp in Berlin."
"But did he tell you, exactly, where he was?" "First he was in
Waldsee [in southern Germany] and then Freisler sent him to
Sachsenhausen." "There is no concentration camp in Waldsee,
and he didn't go to Sachsenhausen. I know that for a fact." "My
aunt Fine [Josefine] was there herself. She witnessed it." "Aunt
Fine was at the trial, and Freisler was the presiding judge. But
he didn't send Joseph to Sachsenhausen. He sent him to Coswig,
which was not a concentration camp." "But the Americans liberated him." "That's true, too. But not from Sachsenhausen.
Not from a concentration camp."

My mother was getting defensive, and I was getting aggressive, until I realized that she was not doubting my research, just
reiterating the stories she had been told, stories that had been
in the family for decades and finally put down on paper by her
aunt Josefine; it was difficult to let these stories go.

I wondered of course whether the Sachsenhausen story developed to exaggerate Joseph's sufferings, or perhaps to show that
the Kresser family had been on the "right side": victims rather
than perpetrators. Kresser himself didn't talk much about his
experience, but he may have told his family of crammed living
quarters, people dying around him, hard labor, and the shoot-
ing of "sexual deviants" by the SS, and this might well have
sounded to farmers from southern Germany, who had never
traveled anywhere, like the stories that were slowly coming out
about concentration camps. Josefine, who had been present at
her father's trial, must have assimilated information about concentration camps into her personal memories and formed them
into a coherent story.

In *The Body Keeps the Score*, his book on trauma, Bessel van der Kolk describes how trauma victims alter their tales over decades of remembering and retelling them: "The act of telling itself changes the tale. The mind cannot help but make meaning out of what it knows, and the meaning we make of our lives changes how and what we remember."[16] This is what Joseph Kresser—and his family—had done over the decades. Oral family stories and archival material: the two are very different ways of relating to the past. The official government documents of the case told a story that is more reliable in all particulars, in the impersonal language of bureaucracy. But the family stories, based on the memories of participants and their children, weren't wrong. They captured the main outlines of Joseph Kresser's life, the mortal danger in which he found himself, the suffering he experienced, and the killings he witnessed.

After the war, Joseph Kresser struggled to be officially recognized as a victim of the Nazi regime. The injustice he had suffered at the hands of Roland Freisler needed to be remedied, especially since Freisler himself was killed in a bombing raid during the last days of the war—too kind a death, without humiliation, without reckoning. Kresser also engaged in a campaign against the neighbor who had denounced him and who continued to live right next door. The neighbor was categorized as a minor fellow traveler of the Nazi regime and forced to do manual labor as a lumberjack. This light punishment compared with what he had suffered enraged Joseph Kresser as a mockery. Then, one day, the hated neighbor was killed by a falling tree. Josefine wrote that the accident happened in late November 1945, exactly one year after my great-grandfather's trial. Justice was finally served.

I considered the two ancestors from my two families. On one

side was the great-grandfather who spoke against the regime and was dragged before Freisler; on the other, the swastika-wearing grandfather who put his scholarly expertise in the service of the regime. One, a simple farmer who wasn't taken in by Nazi propaganda and who correctly predicted how it would end; the other, the son of a low-level business clerk who married the daughter of a high school teacher and who thought that the Nazis would help him break into the ranks of academia.

Perhaps even that is too charitable an interpretation. Perhaps Karl Puchner was more than a mere opportunist. Perhaps he was a true believer, at least when it came to language: that Rotwelsch was dirty; that all of its speakers were thieves; that the very existence of Rotwelsch proved that all Jews were criminals; that the mixing of languages at work in Rotwelsch was a crime in itself. Perhaps he really was convinced that his registries and histories of individual names were creating order and defending German and Germany. What would he say now? No matter what he thought and might have said, the fact remains that it was the simple farmer who ended up on the right side of history, not the doctor of philosophy.

The thing that stays most with me about Joseph Kresser's fate during the Nazi regime is the Sachsenhausen song. Even though I now know that he never went to Sachsenhausen, I can't get the image of him marching with his fellow inmates, holding body and soul together with nothing but a song, out of my mind. Clearly, I had trouble letting go of the story myself, even though I knew it to be false. But who knows: the Sachsenhausen song spread to many Nazi camps and prisons. Perhaps Joseph Kresser sang it after all, as he was being marched in and out of Coswig, grateful that he had been spared the worst.

When I shared some of these thoughts with my mother, she

remembered something interesting: when her brother-in-law, uncle Günter, had learned from her about her family, about Joseph Kresser and his trial in Berlin, he had been so taken with the story that he had asked for the trial documents. He said he wanted to study them and do something with them in the future. This was shortly before his death, and the trial documents were lost in the chaos that followed. (I have since been able to retrieve them from state archives.) What had he wanted to do with them? Would he have compared the histories of the two families? Were these trial documents connected in his mind to Rotwelsch? Was he planning to write something along the lines of what I am writing now?

ROTWELSCH LESSON:
GOING TO PRISON IN ROTWELSCH

Kau = (*koje* = berth)
Kiste = (box)
Kittchen = (from Middle-High German *kiche* = prison)
Klemme
Kühle = (*kehilo* = gathering)
Küse = (Czech, *kut'*)
Leck
Mojabit = (after Moabit, the prison in Berlin that still exists)
Pachulke = (prisoner who works around the house, from Czech *pacholek*, for servant)
Paradies = (Yiddish, *pardes*)
Polsche woche = (literally "a round, or full, week," which means, ironically, an entire month)
Polterbais

Ranzen

Schaflorum

Blauer sarg = (blue coffin = police transport vehicle)

Schlunz = (prison food)

Schul; hohe schul = (prison and penitentiary, respectively)

Schwimmen = (to swim: to be in prison)

Seminar = (seminary, from the Latin *seminarium*)

Stille penne = (quiet shelter)

Tfisse = (Hebrew/Yiddish, *tfise*)

Zuckerbüchse = (sugar box)

Chapter 7

AN ATTIC IN PRAGUE

In the summer of 1968, my parents went to Prague, just a few hundred miles from Nuremberg but separated from it by the Iron Curtain. They were excited about the new atmosphere of openness there. The new Czech leader, Alexander Dubček, had announced a more flexible form of socialism. He vowed to reduce the role of the Communist Party in people's lives, shrink the power of the secret police, pursue less doctrinaire economic policies and abolish censorship.

For several days my parents explored the city, from the medieval castle to the squares with their joyful gatherings of citizens and foreigners who, like my parents, had come here to witness a historical experiment. On the night of August 21, they heard airplanes flying low. The sound reminded my mother of childhood memories from the war. Confused, my parents went outside and asked what was happening. They were told that the invasion of Prague had begun. Russia and its Eastern Bloc allies, especially East Germany, sent a total of 650,000 soldiers, equipped

with heavy war machinery and two thousand tanks, to subdue
this small country and crush its experiment in socialism with a
human face. The people offered no armed resistance, only civil
disobedience and nonviolent resistance. People threw flowers at
tanks and tried to fraternize with the young Russian soldiers.

My father wanted to run out and take pictures, but my mother
persuaded him to pack up and drive to the border immediately.
A mass exodus from the city was under way and traffic was cha-
otic. A stranger guided them through back streets and put them
on the road toward the German border. My parents saw units of
the East German army marching in.

Suddenly they couldn't continue because a Russian tank was
blocking their way. My father cursed and honked. My mother
saw people putting money in their passports before handing
them to the Russians. She got my father to do the same thing.
They were scared of being arrested for attempted bribery, but
it worked, and they were finally let through and made it to the
actual border. On the other side, radio stations were interviewing returning tourists. My father was among them, and his
family learned that my parents had escaped harm by recognizing his voice on the radio.

My father, along with many other Western leftists, responded
to the experience by turning against communism. Watching
the Soviet Union crush these modest gestures of independence
was a deeply disillusioning experience. During his time at the
commune, and of mooning art in Munich's most elegant museums, my father had been on the left, though I am not sure quite
how far left. After the Prague Spring, he moved gradually to
embrace more centrist and even conservative positions.

His most important response to this experience, however,

was to make a book using thick paper and cardboard, held together by spiral binding. The book contained photographs he had taken and developed by hand and poems he had written during and after the trip. It was dedicated to my mother and to the "freedom-loving Czechs and Slovaks." He called it *Prague—1968*.

Some of the poems were an immediate response to his experience, featuring Russian tanks and soldiers who have invaded the city. "Rein in your tanks / soldier / your brother lies in a flower bed / and in his own blood." The longest poem is about a child who points a toy gun at a soldier. Initially the soldier and the child just play a game of fear, but then "those who threaten / and those who feel threatened / have rehearsed their game / for far too long," the trigger is pulled, and the child is dead. My father isn't vilifying the Russian soldiers. They have been trained in sandboxes, he writes, and are now faced with a situation for which they are utterly unprepared. "Where is the memorial / to the unknown soldier who was manipulated?" my father asks.

The photographs, which were paired with the poems, were black-and-white and skillfully developed. Some featured the city's famous cathedrals and synagogues, bridges and castles. Others showed ordinary citizens of Prague, to whom the book is dedicated.

While many of the events he depicted took place in 1968, the book also digs deeper into the history of the city:

> Kafka's Prague
> the city of emperors
> the city with the good acoustics

in the streets
with long echoes
for repetitive sounds
for the crackling of machine guns
The baroque city
the city of the wounded Atlas
who must bear the heavy burden
of balconies
on which Heydrich
may have stood.

My father started with the Russian occupation of 1968 (the "crackling of machine guns," which he himself had heard) but went on to explore the cultural history of the city, highlighting Franz Kafka, who immortalized the city's castle in his novels. Finally, my father turned to the city's Nazi occupation, imagining Reinhard Heydrich, the Nazi ruler of Prague, standing on a balcony. (Heydrich was one of the few high-ranking Nazis to have been successfully assassinated.) My father couldn't look at this beautiful city and its present troubles without thinking of its Nazi past.

The most striking photographs in the book are of Prague's Jewish Cemetery. Some of the images are deliberately overexposed, to turn these ancient stones, gathered together and leaning in every direction, into an Expressionist collage. In some photographs, the tombstones become almost immaterial, transformed into pure light in contrast to the dark trunks of trees, which seem earthbound and heavy. It is a strange, beautiful reversal, stones becoming lighter than trees. The poems accompanying these images ruminate on the history of Judaism.

> Too little room to live
> Even less in death
> Stone upon stone
> Dominoes of persecution

The crowded cemetery mirrors the crowded living conditions of the Prague ghetto, with its narrow streets and people piled upon persecuted people. By the end of the poem, my father worries about tourists (such as himself) crowding around these tombstones, including that of the city's most famous Jewish inhabitant, Rabbi Loew of Prague. "Rabbi Loeb barely has enough room / to turn over in his grave."

My father had engaged with the Jewish Cemetery of Prague and the Nazi occupation of the city around the time that he first discovered his own father's past. In fact, he had used for his Prague book the same equipment with which he had enlarged the family photograph that revealed his father's Nazi allegiance. Photographs and poems: perhaps this was how my father tried to make sense of his inheritance, of what it meant to be a German of a generation just young enough to have escaped personal culpability (my father was born in 1938), but grappling with what it meant to have fathers who had proudly worn swastikas. I couldn't help but feel that the Prague book was his response to his father's misdeeds, his way of coming to terms with the past.

When my mother returned home after my father's death, she found a book of poems at his bedside table. The poems were by Nelly Sachs, a German-Jewish poet from Berlin who had become so terrified after the Nazi takeover that she temporarily lost the ability to speak. She escaped to Sweden in 1940 and began to express what she couldn't say through speech in written poetry. A few days after my father's funeral, my mother gave each of us children a copy of that volume. I take it out and read it now and then, knowing that these were the last words my father read before his death.

The first poem of the volume is called "Dwellings of the Dead."[1] In it, Nelly Sachs asks about chimneys in concentration camps:

> Who thought you up and built you brick by brick
> The routes of escape for migrants made of smoke.

Did my father, as he read these lines, think: I have an answer to this question? Did he say, Yes, it was my father, among many others, who was complicit with these chimneys?

——

As I was leafing through my father's Prague book, memories
of walking with my father through the streets of the city came
flashing back to me. My parents had taken me to Prague in the
late 1980s to introduce me to the city that loomed so large in
their memories. It was my first time behind the Iron Curtain
and I mostly remember how strange and different everything
was, from the cars and clothes to the way people walked and
behaved, how they offered service in restaurants, to their smells
and gestures. My father was less interested in these differences.
He wanted to show me the Prague of Kafka, of Heydrich, and
of 1968. We spent days going to the medieval synagogue and
the Jewish Cemetery, the castle, and the different apartments
inhabited by Kafka. He showed me where he had seen Russian tanks and where there had been blood spilled on the street.
This was his Prague.

Little did I know that this Prague was deeply entangled with
Rotwelsch. I discovered this connection when, handling my
father's book, I decided to return. I took advantage of a work-
shop on Prague literature and found myself there once more,
but this time in the Prague of the mid-1990s, after the fall of
the Iron Curtain, and an influx of Western gold diggers who
had come here to make a quick buck.

The main attraction for me was Prague's most famous writer,
Franz Kafka. I had long admired his fictions of endless trials
and other bureaucratic nightmares, what my father had meant
when he had referred to "Kafka's Prague" in his poem. On the
surface, Kafka's Prague was modern, shaped by the machinery
of the state and its agents, not by medieval cemeteries and ghettos. For most of his life, Kafka worked in an insurance agency.
He was a modern white-collar worker. Above his desk was a

poster containing different body parts with price tags, showing what the insurance would pay for the loss of each limb. The poster captured the cold logic of the world every time Kafka would lift his head.

In his novels, Kafka described this world, but with a twist. Courtrooms, bureaucratic functionaries, lawyers' quarters—they were all connected by secret passageways and staircases, hidden doors and dark corridors, reminiscent of the former Jewish ghetto. People lived on top of one another, waiting rooms giving way to bedrooms, lovers spilling out of broom closets, judges' chambers becoming bedrooms. Kafka, I realized, had turned the particular architecture of his city to new use.

But the center of Kafka's work was language. It was through language that he rebelled against the milieu in which he had grown up, and it was in the course of this rebellion that he encountered Rotwelsch.

When Kafka was growing up, Prague was still part of the Habsburg Empire, which meant that the language of government and culture, used by the middle and upper classes, was German. Kafka came from the bourgeois Jewish milieu, which had long been assimilated into the majority culture of the Austro-Hungarian Empire, especially after being granted emancipation and equal rights. For this process of assimilation, the use of High German, *Hochdeutsch*, was seen as crucial. If there was something the Prague bourgeoisie definitely did not want to be associated with, it was Yiddish, the language of rubes living in shtetls (remote villages), which to them reeked of tradition-bound Jewish life before emancipation, of medieval ignorance and superstition, of everything the Jewish middle class hoped it had left behind. Yiddish theater, in particular, was considered crude and unsophisticated, with starkly drawn characters, simple, melodramatic plots, and exaggerated acting.[2] Many Yiddish playwrights, actors, and directors had come to deplore this state of the art-form and tried to leave behind the reputation for *shund* (trash) and *kitsch* (tasteless, perhaps from Rotwelsch *kitschen*, to buy or sell something that has been stolen), by creating a high-art Yiddish theater.[3]

But Kafka was not bothered by Yiddish *shund*. He had fallen in love with a troupe of Yiddish players, ultimately becoming an ardent supporter, and knew that in order to promote their work, he needed to sell not only their plays and acting styles but also their language. For this purpose, he wrote a lecture that sought to convert German audiences to Yiddish theater. His idea was to tell these German-speaking theater-goers to appreciate Yiddish as a language that sounded strange to them, but underneath that strangeness they would discover an unexpected similarity. (This had been exactly my experience as well.) Kafka's view was an interesting variation on the old, and false, story about Yiddish as a secret language. Instead of harping on incomprehensibility, Kafka said that engaging with Yiddish made something strange familiar.

Kafka also described Yiddish as a mobile language that captured the experience of centuries of migration. From his German-speaking perspective, Yiddish sounded as if words and expressions had moved from their preassigned place in the language, shifting sideways in pronunciation, meaning, and syntax. It was a wayward language. Kafka praised this mobility as a way of creating new expressions and layers of association. He even thought that Yiddish might revitalize German, or as he put it, "rake up" German, as if the language were a lawn that needed to be aerated.

In praising Yiddish, Kafka referred to the language as "jargon," using the French word for something incomprehensible, similar to the word *welsch* in Rotwelsch. Kafka didn't mind the negative connotations. He liked the fact that Yiddish would inject something incomprehensible into German, even while he also tried to convince his audience that they would understand it somehow. Jargon was good.

In the course of praising Yiddish as the unruly offspring of German, Kafka came across Rotwelsch.[4] This "thieves' cant," as he called it, was a language even stranger, more mobile, and more *welsch*, than Yiddish: the Yiddish of Yiddish. And here, Kafka extended his argument about Yiddish: even though Rotwelsch could be seen as incomprehensible and secret, it could evoke in readers the same experience of familiarity and estrangement that could be obtained in Yiddish, perhaps even more so. In his enthusiastic praise of Yiddish, Kafka overemphasizes its mobility, its lack of grammar or rules (Yiddish does have a grammar and rules). But while his characterization of Yiddish is slightly questionable, what he said about Yiddish is actually true of Rotwelsch.

Inspired by Kafka, I began to research the local language and realized that Prague had in fact developed its own variant of Rotwelsch, one with more Czech words, part of the process that had led Rotwelsch from the road to the underground of cities such as Prague and Vienna (where Hitler would have encountered it).[5] Prague had even acquired a Rotwelsch name: Bandl-Foro.

Rotwelsch changed when it moved from the countryside into the city. Whereas previously it had contained expressions drawn from agriculture and the foods that could be stolen or obtained by begging, now it was dominated by the demands of the urban underground such as playing cards, organizing prostitution, and planning elaborate heists.⁶ Living on the road was becoming rarer, even though contact with the police remained frequent, and therefore expressions connected to it persisted. There was an increase in *zinken* to be found in Prague over the course of the nineteenth century, as a scholar by the name of Puchmayer noted.⁷

What had begun as a trip to follow in my father's footsteps had brought me back to Rotwelsch. Even better: for once Rotwelsch wasn't looked down upon, at least not by Kafka. This was an important change. Kafka himself continued writing in High German and didn't use Yiddish or Rotwelsch in his novels and essays, nor did he let those languages infiltrate his German.⁸ For all his rebellion, he, too, was a product of Jewish assimilation (although he also had an interest in Zionism and studied Hebrew). But while he didn't practice what he preached when it came to Yiddish, he recognized Rotwelsch as a cultural phenomenon to be cherished, and as a resource for theater and literature.

===

My father loved another building in Prague: the strangely named Old-New Synagogue. The teacher of the summer course on Prague literature I was taking led me up a set of winding stairs to the attic, the most famous part of the entire old structure. I found, to my great surprise, that this building was connected to Rotwelsch as well—through the Kabbalah, the mystical science of secret names and symbols in the Hebrew Bible and elsewhere.

A sacred text was believed to contain many more meanings than were obvious on the surface. Kabbalists developed elaborate methods of reading between the lines, pondering unusual

meanings of individual letters and words, or combining names and letters to reveal hidden meanings put there by God and open only to the most ingenious of interpreters. At the center of this science were the secret names of God. Originally an oral tradition, Kabbalah became a rich and versatile practice in which initiates could excel by poring over single lines and words with great intensity. Every combination of letters and words was significant.

One person who became closely associated with the Kabbalah was Judah Loew ben Bezalel, also known as Rabbi Loew. A sixteenth-century philosopher, he believed in the hidden meanings of the Hebrew Bible. (I finally understood the reference in my father's poem about the Jewish Cemetery: "Rabbi Loeb barely has enough room / to turn over in his grave.") According to legend, he also created the Golem, a clay figure brought to life through a recitation of a secret name of God, made to protect the Jews of Prague against anti-Semites. The attic of the Old-New Synagogue was the Golem's dwelling place, the reason it had become the epicenter of Kabbalistic Prague.

Rabbi Loew, the Kabbalah, and Rotwelsch were all brought together by a lesser-known contemporary of Kafka, the best-selling author of *The Golem*: Gustav Meyrink.[9] In this novel, Meyrink turned Rotwelsch into something like the Kabballah's low-life twin. The connection made sense to me. Like the Kabballah, Rotwelsch dealt in secret names, even though they were secret names of thieves, not of God, and like the Kabbalah Rotwelsch used signs that looked benign—but for those versed in their meaning, those signs could reveal an entire hidden world. If the Kabbalah represented the mysteries of language for religious interpretation, Rotwelsch represented the mysteries of language for the life of the underground.

Meyrink was not the first to make this connection. As early as 1620, an author from Nuremberg, hiding behind the pseudonym Resene Gibronte Runeclus Hanedi, wrote a comprehensive treatise on cryptology. It included the art of communicating secretly with the help of optical and acoustic devices as well as methods of sending letters secretly, using ciphers and special inks.[10] (The pseudonym of the author was encrypted as well: it is an anagram, rearranging the letters of his name in Latin, Daniel Schuuenterus Norimbergensis.) Not content with mere encryption keys, Daniel Schwenter of Nuremberg (in the German spelling of his name) also waded into deeper waters, including different Kabbalistic sign systems. They weren't used for secret communication between people, but secret messages from God, to be decrypted by the few who had mastered this obscure art. In the minds of these writers, deciphering messages from God and deciphering messages from criminals were connected because they both depended on the idea of a secret language and secret signs. The highest and the lowest were intriguingly related.

It was in this context that Schwenter came across Rotwelsch and incorporated it into his treatise. Drawing on Luther and other sources, he recognized Rotwelsch as a combination of different languages, but emphasized Hebrew as a dominant one (after German). He particularly noted that the Rotwelsch term for god was the Hebrew Adonai, a point that resonated with the Kabbalistic interest in the names of God. But more important than this connection was the idea of secrecy. Schwenter reports a scene that would be repeated over and over again to show Rotwelsch as a secret language used for nefarious purposes. Two soldiers, sitting in a bar, plot to steal. A maid, who knows Rotwelsch, has overheard them, and calmly tells them, in Rotwelsch, to go packing. Surprised and embarrassed, the soldiers leave. The implication is that you need to learn some Rotwelsch in order to understand criminals, just as you need to learn Kabbalah in order to understand God.

Rotwelsch kept popping up in unexpected places. More and more it seemed like a screen onto which different people could project different things: conspiracies and plots; hidden underground worlds; the life of the road; and, now, Kabbalistic signs and symbols.

ROTWELSCH LESSON:
KAFKA'S FAVORITE KOCHEMER LOSHN OF BANDL-FORO

The Czech thieves' language called Hantyrka includes Rotwelsch expressions:

Enaien = eyes (Hebrew, *einayim*)
Gifar = village (Hebrew)

Handeln = to steal (German: to trade)
Chafer = pig (Yiddish, *khazer*)
Kaporn = to die (comes from slaughtering animals to celebrate Yom Kippur)
Keim = Jew
Masern = to betray
Masamaten faßern (or *baldowern*) = scouting for a break-in (from Yiddish *masamatn* for purse of money, and *fetzen*, *facere*, to make, in Latin)
Moos = money
Schiebes machen = to escape
Schmosen = to chat

Sample Sentence, Using English as a Base

We were in a gifar near Bandl-Foro because a keim was kaporn, when we enaien someone about to masern us for a bit of moos. Immediately, we faßern a masamaten. Tonight, the handel will go well.

Chapter 8

WHEN JESUS SPOKE ROTWELSCH

—————

My discoveries of the literary uses of Rotwelsch by Kafka and Meyrink gave me an inkling of what my uncle might have been up to. I tried to arrange Günter's publications and the contents of his archive chronologically to get a better sense of how his interest in Rotwelsch had evolved. His earliest experiments were translations—into Rotwelsch. He began with the New Testament. First, my uncle created his own compilation of Bible passages based on Luther's Bible, perhaps as payback for Luther's campaign against the Welsh cant of beggars. He arranged scenes from the four Gospels into a chronological narrative, what is called a synoptic Bible. It was something church authorities had done in the past to smooth out repetitions and contradictions between the gospel writers, as none of the four were actual eyewitnesses to the events they were describing. The church was invested in turning the life of Jesus into a single authoritative narrative. More recently, individual writers had also tried their hands at creating a synoptic Bible,

above all the devout Russian author Leo Tolstoy, who hoped
that this new version of the Gospels would be the basis for a
return to a simpler and purer form of Christianity.

My uncle had other plans for his synoptic Bible. It began
with the birth of Jesus according to Luke, continued with
the Marriage at Cana, from John, and went on to Matthew's
description of Jesus walking across water, all in Rotwelsch. At
first, I thought he simply wanted to shock God-fearing Christians by translating scripture into a thieves' cant, the linguistic
version of mooning religion. But that wasn't it at all. His translation actually brought out the irreverence of the New Testament, the fact that it praised the lowest of the low, the outcasts,
not the scribes and religious leaders. A good example was the
scene on the cross: *"No schmuste er zum Joisl: Hoh, holm an minz,
wenn du in deine Glut baust. Und der Joisl perlte zu ihm: Nebbich,
ich pleißle dir, hajom wirst du mit mir im Ganeden sein."*[1] This was
my uncle's translation of the moment when one of the thieves
says: "Remember me when you come into your kingdom," and
Jesus replies: "Truly I tell you, today you will be with me in
paradise."

My uncle was having fun. Perhaps he thought that Jesus
would have been happy to be caught shmoozing (or schmusing,
as my uncle spelled it) with one of the thieves in Rotwelsch. It
made me think of the writer in Gog's *The Vagrant* who considered Jesus the original wanderer and outcast. How fitting that
Jesus was now using the language of the road.

For a German speaker, some words in these Rotwelsch sentences would be familiar, but most of them wouldn't. My uncle
hoped that his readers might remember the passage in the original and glean its meaning in Rotwelsch. Because Rotwelsch
used a good number of German words and German-based

Yiddish words, reading this translated Bible wasn't exactly like reading a completely foreign language; it was more like reading a familiar story in a new, estranged idiom (exactly what Kafka had claimed for Yiddish). The point of the exercise wasn't to undermine the Bible but to allow Günter's readers to experience it in a new way. Günter didn't intend to drag the Bible down; he wanted to lift Rotwelsch up.

By hoping to turn Rotwelsch into a literary language, my uncle was taking inspiration from the century-long campaign to have Yiddish recognized as its own language. How different was Yiddish from various spoken German dialects? On the face of it, Yiddish looked very different because it was written with Hebrew letters, from right to left (which had fueled the charge of secrecy). But aside from the writing system, the actual vocabulary and grammar were predominantly German.

The works in my uncle's archive suggested that the distinction between a dialect and a language came down not so much to linguistic difference as to prestige. Among his books I found one by the great Yiddish scholar Max Weinreich, who complained that Yiddish wasn't taken seriously because it didn't have the power of a state behind it. The insight was based on a remark someone had made to him after a lecture, now a standard trope: "A language is a dialect with an army and a navy."[2]

Günter's close study of Yiddish was beginning to make sense to me: it offered guidance for his own campaign of rescuing Rotwelsch from obscurity and giving it new prestige. This was precisely what advocates of Yiddish had done. Instead of enlisting military support, they standardized Yiddish grammar by eliminating regional variants and other elements associated with purely spoken language. Then they made every effort to write in Yiddish. This put them in direct competition with

Hebrew, which had hitherto been the language used for writing, above all any writing connected to religion and religious life. Because knowledge of Hebrew was, for the most part, reserved for men, early writings in Yiddish, from the seventeenth and eighteenth centuries, were directed at women—or pretended to be. Savvy writers realized that by writing in Yiddish and claiming that they were writing for women, they could reach a larger audience, an audience not only of women but of less-educated men as well.[3] Soon enough, written Yiddish was everywhere, in newspapers and other printed matter used in everyday life.

Günter was not content with these findings. He dug deeper into the history of Yiddish and was particularly interested in its enemies, inspired no doubt by his experience with Rotwelsch and its plentiful detractors, including his own father. In the case of Yiddish, however, there weren't just anti-Semitic enemies to contend with but also groups within the Jewish community. Many rabbis and Bible scholars dismissed Yiddish as the language of everyday life and unfit for higher uses, like literature. Equally opposed to Yiddish, but for different reasons, were some of those advocating a return to Palestine. While a number of early Zionists imagined a Jewish state with German as its official language, others believed that in Palestine Jews would revert to Hebrew as the language of everyday life. (Against all odds, the latter position prevailed, even though the settlers had to create a modern version of Hebrew first.) Finally, there were those who recommended assimilation, urging Jews to adopt the language of the majority population.

Despite these external and internal enemies, Yiddish expanded over the course of the eighteenth, nineteenth, and early twentieth centuries, and as Günter discovered, one weapon proved particularly important for its defense: literature.

To this end, the promoters of Yiddish translated texts into Yiddish, laying the foundation for a new literature.

The strategy worked. One sign of success came in 1925, when Weinreich and others founded YIVO (Yidisher Visenshaftlekher Institut), an institute headquartered in Vilnius that assumed the work of regulating Yiddish much like the esteemed Académie Française regulated French. Even though YIVO didn't have the power of a state behind it, it became a well-regarded research institute, seeking to create a "Yiddish science," scholarship in and about Yiddish. YIVO still exists today—it is now based in New York—continuing the work on behalf of Yiddish that had begun so many centuries ago with translations of the Bible and other texts.

Günter had drawn an important lesson from this history: if you don't have an army and a navy to turn your dialect into a language, translate literature, preferably the Bible.

===

Inspired by what he had learned about Yiddish and its successful program of literary translation, my uncle expanded the range of his translations into Rotwelsch. After the Bible, his next target was Shakespeare: *Hippiger Romeo!* . . . *O gable lau beim Bleck, dem Überbeuter / der merwig seinen Rädling wawert / damit den Rauch dein Lenzen wawerbar!*[4] Yes, *hippiger* reader, it is the balcony scene from *Romeo and Juliet.* Apparently, Rotwelsch wasn't just the language of the thieves on the cross but also the language of love. *Hippiger,* for dear, came from the Yiddish *chiba.* The next word, *gable,* was derived from the German word for fork (*Gabel*), but in Rotwelsch it meant to swear because the prongs of a fork looked like the fingers of a hand raised when swearing an oath. *Bleck* was based on the Czech word *pleck*, for silver coin, but in Rotwelsch it referred to the moon. Passages such as these brought out the wit of Rotwelsch, which took everyday objects such as silver coins for romantic moons and connected an oath with a utensil.

In all likelihood, nobody ever talked that way. My uncle, after all, wasn't translating these texts for Rotwelsch speakers. Instead he was creating a new literary language.

After the Bible and Shakespeare, there was no stopping him. He ranged widely in literary history, both high and low, translating an eighteenth-century conduct manual instructing young gentlemen how to address ladies, a Sicilian fairy tale, a lullaby, numerous short stories, and journalistic articles as well as a short text on Marxism and Christianity, perhaps out of deference for Gog's time in the Soviet Union. All of these texts Günter painstakingly translated into Rotwelsch, a language only he could read. The absurdity of his undertaking haunted me. What could have been the purpose of this doomed translation exercise?

In his attempt to create a Rotwelsch world literature, Günter undid the work of Luther, generations of policemen, and his own father, all of whom had hoped to keep German free from Rotwelsch. By translating works from English, German, Spanish, Hebrew, and Greek into Rotwelsch for a German readership (he always printed German translations on a facing page), he tried to let this thieves' cant loose on German.

My uncle was determined to see his translation project through to completion. He located a publisher willing to take on the book and spent large amounts of time specifying its layout, which was complicated because the *zinken* had to be drawn by hand. Once he held the published book, titled *Kundenschall*

(Kochemer Sounds), in his hands, he was thrilled, and he did everything he could to promote it. He split the printing and binding costs with the publisher and sent copies to everyone he knew. He even had a few positive reviews. In later negotiations with another publisher, he claimed that the book had sold three thousand copies—an exaggeration perhaps, but even if he sold only half as many, the book could be described as a notable success, given its arcane subject matter.

===

Among the masterworks of world literature, my uncle had seized on the most canonical German author, Johann Wolfgang von Goethe, and translated a scene from his play *Faust* in which the wronged Gretchen is praying to God. Did Günter do this because he knew that Goethe had pioneered the term "world literature," the idea that the great works of literature should be understood not according to national traditions but as part of a single world culture?

Goethe wrote at a time when many German writers were searching out German traditions and folkways, seeking to combat the influence of French literature on their culture. But Goethe didn't like this turn to nationalism and was casting about for an alternative. He came up with one alternative on the afternoon of January 31, 1827. That day, Johann Peter Eckermann, his faithful secretary, went to Goethe's house in the provincial town of Weimar, as he had done hundreds of times in the past three and a half years. Goethe reported on what he had read since they last talked. Apparently, he had been reading a Chinese novel.[5] "Really? That must have been rather strange!" Eckermann exclaimed. "Much less so than one

thinks," Goethe replied.[6] Eckermann was surprised and ven-
tured that surely this Chinese novel must be quite unusual,
the exception to the rule. Wrong again. The master's voice was
stern: "Nothing could be further from the truth. The Chinese
have thousands of them, and had them when our ancestors
were still living in the woods." Eckermann was confused, but
Goethe wasn't done yet and reached for the term that would
stun his secretary: "The era of world literature is at hand, and
everyone must contribute to accelerating it."[7] World literature
was born out of this debate with the narrow-minded Eckermann. Goethe wished to redirect European readers to read
more widely, across cultures. As it happens, Yiddish was one
of his interests—in his youth, he had worked on an epistolary
novel partly written in Yiddish.[8]

Since Goethe, world literature had become a rallying cry
of those advocating on behalf of smaller, non-established literatures, including Yiddish. One of them was Melech Ravitch,
who called himself the first Yiddish modernist. In 1936, he
declared that there existed a Yiddish *velt literatur* (world literature).[9] By this he meant that Yiddish was a literature written in
different parts of the world, from Eastern Europe to the United
States. But he also meant that it was something to aspire to:
Yiddish writers should be able to gain a place in world literature
even though they were being ignored by the majority cultures
of Europe. To this end, Ravitch translated many works of world
literature, including Franz Kafka, into Yiddish. World literature promised a path to literary prominence outside the metro-
politan centers of cultural power.

Günter pursued a similar project. Instead of making narrow-
minded German readers read Chinese novels or Persian poetry,
as Goethe had done, he wanted them to read Rotwelsch litera-

ture, persuading them that all around them there existed a kind of underground world literature that he, Günter, was now presenting for the first time.

There was one problem: there wasn't any Rotwelsch literature to begin with. Perhaps my uncle thought that by translating snippets of great scenes *from* world literature, he might jump-start the process by which, at some point in the future, there might actually be a Rotwelsch literature the way there already existed one in Yiddish.

But his deepest motivation must have been something else. Günter had taken up Rotwelsch just around the time his brother, my father, had told him about their father's Nazi past.

Perhaps Günter's plunge into Rotwelsch was atonement—or something closer to revenge. He mentions several times that Yiddish and Rotwelsch speakers had been sent to concentration camps. The accusatory tone is palpable. The fact that he had put his father's copy of *Mein Kampf* among his Rotwelsch books points in the same direction. My father had said that no one in the family knew about my grandfather's anti-Semitic articles, including the one that talks about Rotwelsch. My cousins believe that their father was drawn to the language solely because of its lightness and wit. But I can't shake the hunch that somehow my uncle must have known about his father's opposition to the language. The alternative seemed even stranger: that he would have, almost instinctively, stumbled on the topic his father hated most. Even if Günter didn't know that his father objected to Rotwelsch and that this objection was connected to his father's compromised past, Günter's dedication to Rotwelsch would have served a more general, historical atonement, atonement for a regime that had tried to eliminate the language and its speakers.

It now also made sense that among the texts Günter had translated into Rotwelsch was the German national anthem. Later, I found out that the poet who composed the lyrics actually had a lively interest in Rotwelsch and recognized its "poetic" potential—Rotwelsch kept haunting German national identity.[10] Clearly, Günter had intuited the same thing as he grappled with Nazism, both on a national level and on a personal one. His campaign on behalf of Rotwelsch and his father's past were connected.

━━

Even though Günter saw his translation project into print, he didn't pursue it further. But this didn't mean he had given up on Rotwelsch. Instead he continued using Rotwelsch in his own poetry for another ten years, until the moment of his sudden death.

Perhaps inspired by his translation of a scene from *Romeo and Juliet*, Günter initially focused his Rotwelsch-infused poetry on love. His goal, as he explained in a letter to a prospective publisher, was to strip love of anything that would sound conventional. "Carnal love is often used as a substitute for real communication," he observed. His collection would revolve around tenderness, human warmth, and constancy. Another reason for our failure to communicate, he added, was worn-out words. "Out of fear and indifference—to protect ourselves— we hold on to empty, formulaic, prefabricated words that don't express what we mean but that are deemed good enough."[11] The poems were part of his campaign to destroy the clichés we use as shields to keep others away.

To break our habit of using pat words, Günter proposed

replacing them with words from unusual dialects and languages, including Yiddish and Rotwelsch. Rotwelsch allowed him to capture sensual impressions with much greater precision and plasticity than normal German, he explained. Worn formulations would be enlivened, calcified clichés burst open, giving way to vivid expressions with infinite gradations and meanings. Günter was repeating Kafka's goal that Yiddish and Rotwelsch would "rake up" German, with the hope not of secrecy and incomprehension, but instead of better, fuller communication.

Günter's letter to the publisher was returned a few weeks later unanswered, but eventually he did find a publisher for this collection of Rotwelsch-infused love poetry. Producing the book was a nightmare because my uncle wanted to include not only Rotwelsch words written in the Roman alphabet but also Hebrew words and other unusual graphic elements, including drawings of celestial constellations. Günter also got into a fight with his publisher about the paper, the type of gray used on the cover, and other production details.

His efforts were worth it. The book looks unusual with its flexible gray cover that's made out of a deliberately coarse stock.[12] But what I like best about the book is the cover image. It's the portrait of my father I love so much.

The two brothers had their differences. I was too young to know the details, or rather, I had not been told and had not asked. When I talked to my mother about this recently, she said: "I didn't get involved in things like that." (Notverynice things, I thought.) In retrospect, I think that whatever differences existed between the brothers had to do with their changing life circumstances, with my uncle's continuing a form of bohemian life while my father became more bourgeois. Despite these differences, my uncle put the portrait of my father on the

cover of his book of love poems. Perhaps he felt that communication between himself and his brother, too, was hampered by clichés and imprecise words. The brothers had had additional quarrels, even a temporary falling-out over some aspect of their inheritance. Perhaps Günter was trying to communicate by other means, through poems and the choice of his cover art.

My uncle called the collection *An Armful of Schmonzes,* using the Yiddish (and Rotwelsch) word for idle talk. An armful of chatter. I find it a charmingly modest title, given his lofty goal of reviving true communication. The poems are challenging but evocative, above all one called "The Yenish Festival in the Clouds." Yenish was a word for the thieves' argot spoken in Swabia and Switzerland in the nineteenth century, part of the Rotwelsch family of jargons (because Rotwelsch was a mobile, spoken language, it kept changing and acquiring new names). Why did my uncle locate his Yenish festival in the clouds? The poem describes a street fair taking place in Munich, the type of gathering that might have attracted professional travelers selling trinkets.

Günter soon planned an entire collection around this title. In a letter to yet another prospective publisher, he explained his enduring infatuation with Rotwelsch in new ways. Now he suggested that he wanted to escape our materialistic world by opening himself up to the Other, and in terms of language, the Other was Rotwelsch. Rotwelsch allowed him to enter another world, a world different from his own. Capturing that world in a new language would make it possible for him and his readers to interrupt the routines of their lives—including their routine use of language.

Günter died before he was able to find a publisher. When I started reading his manuscripts and typewritten drafts, which he kept changing just as he kept changing the sequence of poems, I realized that this collection constituted the culmination of his Rotwelsch career. It was based on a lifelong dream that he had finally made a reality: to travel to Israel.

Most of the poems collected under the title *Yenish Festival in the Clouds* were a poetic travelogue of his experience in Jerusalem and at the Red Sea. The time was April 1982. Israel had just fought a war in southern Lebanon and officially withdrawn, but there were frequent skirmishes. In May, Israel would invade southern Lebanon again, forcing Palestinians to retreat farther north, to Beirut. In September, Christian Phalangists from Lebanon would kill hundreds of Palestinians in the refugee camps of Sabra and Shatila.

Violence was rife in Israel, and Günter was disturbed by it. It shaped everything he saw, from everyday tourist preoccupations—the price of breakfast—to conversations with a female travel companion as well as with soldiers and ordinary people he met. Violence even shaped the cultural landmarks

such as the Wailing Wall, the Temple Mount, and Bethlehem—
"Uphill toward Bethlehem / Where the Testaments meet /
Coronation of the Apes." Standing at one of the hot spots of
civilization, my uncle wasn't impressed. The Judeo-Christian-
Islamic traditions, with their sacred texts and testaments, had
much to answer for.

I could tell from the poems that the highlight of the trip, for
him, was when he overheard an exchange in a bar. A young soldier enters and removes the magazine from his rifle, as required
in indoor spaces. *"Nebbich, ich wer eich ersaifn, ihr Bestiess, ihr
varfluchte!"* (So what, I'm going to drown you, you beasts, damn
you.) It was a fragment of a heated discussion. The language, as
rendered by my uncle, wasn't Yiddish, exactly. Rather, it was a
strange concoction of Yiddish (*nebbich* for *nebekh*) and Bavarian
(*ersaifn*; *varfluchte*). It gave me the feeling that what he had been
searching for in Israel was not the monuments, the layers of history, or the political tensions, but remnants of a language that
his father had loathed.

The publisher wasn't interested in a collection of poems
called *Yenish Festival in the Clouds* that reported on my uncle's
hunt for Yiddish words. I don't know whether my uncle tried
other publishers; I found no such record among his papers.
Then suddenly he was dead, and his wife moved everything
into the attic. There the poems remained until I came looking
for clues about my grandfather and Rotwelsch.

I now had before me the arc of Günter's work. It began with
the literary journal, took a turn to Rotwelsch with his massive
research and translation project, and ended with his attempted
infusion of Rotwelsch and Yiddish into German. What had
looked to me like an eccentric hobby, then an obsession, turned
out to be a serious undertaking with a purpose.

ROTWELSCH LESSON:
A QUIXOTIC ATTEMPT TO CREATE ROTWELSCH
LITERATURE (TRANSLATION BY GÜNTER PUCHNER)

"Welche Wütlinge," schalte Sancho Pansa.

"Die du kannst raunst" schuffte sein Sens, "mit den schleffen Schlufen, die küstig wui zwis Ellen grimm sind. . . ."

Mit dieser Dresche störte er dem Süßchen Rosinante die Spitzeln, bi auf die Kille seines Stänkergeists zu lustern, der ihm mei dicki nachhallte, daß es nebbich Püfferrollen und tschi Grimmlinge schäften, was er angriffeln wähnte.

"Which giants?" asked Sancho Panza.

"Those that you can see over there," answered his master, "with their gigantic arms, which must be two miles long. . . ."

With these words, he spurred on his horse Rosinante, without listening to the voice of his stableman, who called after him, that those were certainly windmills and not giants with which he wanted to battle.

Chapter 9

IGPAY ATINLAY FOR ADULTS

———

Sometimes, when he was in a good mood, my father would say something that sounded like *kakao mada dapish.* "Dad, what are you saying?!" "Oh, you didn't understand? I am speaking Esperanto." My brother and I would giggle and imitate the sounds he had made: "*kookoo mada dada.*" "Very good," he would say, "only it's *dapish*, not *dada.*"

"It's a universal language," he would explain. "Everyone can understand it. Listen: *kakao mada dapish.*" We would try to answer, pretending that we were fluent in this strange language, whatever it was, before we would get bored and run away. Did we mind that we couldn't understand a word? I don't think so. It was simply another language game, something to goof around with, another thing to do with words.

I don't know why my father was intrigued by Esperanto. He didn't say much about it and only played his Esperanto game with us from time to time. Once, when we were visiting a church in northern Italy, he pointed to a group of tourists who were speaking in a language I couldn't understand. "They're speaking Esperanto," he declared. "Really? An Esperanto tour group? We want to see it!" we shouted and ran over to eavesdrop. The results were inconclusive. Very likely, there were no Esperanto tour groups in northern Italy or anywhere else. Why did he create this elaborate fiction that we could speak Esperanto and that others did as well? Only later did it occur to me that his Esperanto sentences were probably made up as well. At least I remember them only as sequences of funny sounds.

My father also never said anything about the history of Esperanto, but I sensed that it was connected to the threads I had been isolating in the tapestry of his life: his brother's fascination with Rotwelsch, the literary journal the brothers had edited, and poetry. Like Günter, my father was thinking about communication, the difficulties of saying what he wanted to say and what he might leave behind in his nocturnal poetry.

Esperanto—the name means hopeful (in Esperanto)—was the creation of Ludwig Zamenhof, who had grown up in the multilingual cacophony of late-nineteenth-century Białystok, in today's Poland, speaking Russian, German, and Yiddish.[1] His fascination with language began in his teens, when he tried to make Yiddish, especially its grammar, which was based on the conveniences of everyday speech, more systematic and orderly. He was among those who hoped to turn Yiddish into a language that would be recognized on a par with others. At this point in his career, Zamenhof resembled the many Yiddish advocates I had encountered in my uncle's archive. Even though Yiddish was gaining ground as a written language—a development my uncle would later study as a model for Rotwelsch—Zamenhof's attempt to standardize the grammar of Yiddish failed miserably. The conclusion he drew from this experience was that since it was impossible to rationalize existing languages, they were better left alone. Instead, he would construct a new one.

Zamenhof wasn't the first to dream of a new language that would be free from all the inherited anomalies that had driven him crazy with Yiddish: rules that didn't always apply, verbs that didn't behave as they should, and other ways in which actually existing languages were, from his perspective, simply a mess. It was a miracle that people could make themselves understood at all. Faced with such chaos, language philosophers, linguistic engineers, and well-meaning reformers had tried their hands at constructing new languages, coming up with impressively logical but otherwise useless proposals.

Yet for Zamenhof, the purpose of Esperanto wasn't order for its own sake; it was to facilitate communication across language barriers. If humans were all able to communicate with one another, and had one language in common, human strife would disappear. The tragedy of Babel, when God punished humans' arrogance by confusing their tongues, would come to an end. The tower could be rebuilt because Esperanto would facilitate cooperation on an entirely new level. For his building blocks, Zamenhof used the European languages that he knew. But how could he hope to establish his new language?

The crux turned out to be, once again, literature. Originally, Zamenhof had shied away from literary aspirations since his language was meant for clear communication, not the obscure effects of poetry. But over time he relented. He realized Esperanto needed to acquire prestige, and the prestige of languages was conferred by their literature. Like my uncle, he started by translating Shakespeare, the only difference being that instead of *Romeo and Juliet*, Zamenhof chose *Hamlet*. Soon other works followed, especially plays, which could be performed at Esperanto meetings. The first world congress on Esperanto, in 1905, took place in Boulogne, and featured a production of Molière's *Le Mariage forcé* in Esperanto. If the French delegates would accept a production of their favorite playwright in Esperanto, there was hope for the language.

Zamenhof's most ambitious translation project, however, was the Bible. *En la komenco Dio kreis la ĉielon kaj la teron. Kaj la tero estis senforma kaj dezerta, kaj mallumo estis super la abismo; kaj la spirito de Dio ŝvebis super la akvo.* (In the beginning, God created the heaven and the earth. And the earth was without form, and void; and darkness was upon the abyss. And the Spirit of God moved above the waters.) Zamenhof used as his source Moses Mendelssohn's translation of the Hebrew Bible into High German (with which Mendelssohn had tried to counter the Yiddish Bible in order to create an assimilated and, to his mind, enlightened form of Judaism). Later, dedicated Esperantists produced translations of the Christian Old and New Testaments, mostly modeled on the King James Bible.

All this sounded familiar to me because it was so similar to my uncle's Rotwelsch translation of the Bible. I decided to take Esperanto and use it to look at my uncle's project. When I squinted, my uncle's Rotwelsch looked like a low-class version of my father's Esperanto. The difference mapped onto that between my bourgeois father and his bohemian brother.

There was one crucial difference between Rotwelsch and Esperanto: Esperanto wasn't the sociolect of a specific milieu. It was more like the opposite, a language explicitly designed to create open, transparent communication among all humanity. And yet, I felt that Esperanto allowed me to see something new about Rotwelsch. For the people of the road, Rotwelsch facilitated, rather than hindered, communication; Rotwelsch and its *zinken* were meant to be understood by all kinds of people at the bottom of society. It was nobody's first language but an entire milieu's second language, which signaled that its speakers belonged to a distinct group—something like the universal language of the underground.

Pursuing this thought further, I remembered that there were extreme differences between the various dialects of German spoken across Central Europe, dialects that retained their local distinctions for centuries, often to the point of being incomprehensible to one another. It was only the mass media of the twentieth century—above all, radio and television—that sharply reduced these differences, as also happened with other languages and their dialects around the world.

In this patchwork of dialects, Rotwelsch stood out because it combined dialects from across Central Europe. Rotwelsch spoken in the north contained terms typical of Bavaria, in the south, and Rotwelsch from the Rhine, in the west, could be found as far east as Vienna and Prague. This made sense since its speakers were constantly on the road, often traversing regions that most of their inhabitants rarely left. When seen from this perspective, this language of the road was a transregional means of communication, a low form of Esperanto.

Among Kafka's notes, I found a single line that stuck with me: "We are digging the shaft of Babel."[2] At the time, I didn't know what Kafka meant, but after seeing Rotwelsch through the lens of Esperanto, I had an inkling. While Zamenhof tried to rebuild the Tower of Babel with a universal language that would allow for new forms of human cooperation, Kafka and my uncle envisioned something very different: a project of digging into the roots of language. They were attempting to do more than simply rake up words. They were burrowing in hopes of unearthing another, more obscure common language, the lingua franca of the underworld.

It turned out that I wasn't the only one to make this connection between Rotwelsch and Esperanto, although unfortunately it was enemies of Rotwelsch who also noticed this affinity, not a company I was happy to keep. Among my sources, I found a hypernationalist newspaper in Hungary, one of the centers of the Esperanto movement, that attacked Esperanto (just as my Nazi grandfather had attacked Yiddish) for its kinship to Rotwelsch.[3] Rotwelsch, Yiddish, and Esperanto attracted the same anti-Semitic projections.[4] In their hate-filled imagination, anti-Semites had recognized that all three languages were connected to migration in Central Europe. Yiddish was the everyday language of Jewish populations, Esperanto had been invented by a Jewish linguist with an interest in Yiddish, and Rotwelsch included Hebrew words. This, of course, didn't mean that Esperanto and Rotwelsch were "Jewish" languages—nor that this association would be a bad thing—but one couldn't expect anti-Semites to sort out these subtle differences.

Zamenhof's ancestry alone would have been enough to prejudice Hitler against Esperanto when he ranted against the language in *Mein Kampf*. But Hitler also objected to the purpose of Esperanto: that it would facilitate trade, international organizations, and a global labor movement, all of which he identified as a Jewish conspiracy against good German businesses. Nonetheless, there was a brief moment when German nationalists, thinking that some sort of international language was needed, found it convenient to promote Esperanto as an alternative to the enemy languages of French and English; they even formed an SA (Storm Trooper) chapter dedicated to the language.

But the alliance between the Nazis and Esperanto was short-lived. When Hitler was voted into power in 1933, he decried Esperanto as a Jewish-Marxist plot and promoted a German-only policy. Esperanto (like Rotwelsch) was Jewish, Marxist, international, and cosmopolitan—in short, everything he was against. He outlawed the movement.

Esperanto survived Hitler, even though today it has few speakers. In 1971, the *Voyager 1* spacecraft was shot out into space bearing a golden record with greetings in fifty-five languages, a true homage to Babel. Among them was a message in Esperanto: *Ni strebas vivi en paco kun la popoloj de la tuta mondo, de la tuta kosmo,* which meant: "We strive to live in peace with the peoples of the whole world, of the whole cosmos," a fitting greeting for a language designed for universal understanding and peace. *Voyager 1* is still on its way. Let us hope that should it ever encounter intelligent life, its Esperanto message of universal understanding and peace will be understood and honored.

==

Esperanto reminds me of one of the last fights I had with my father—and we had very few of them. When I was in college, I studied Rudolf Carnap, a language philosopher of the early twentieth century who wanted to combat religion and other irrational beliefs, as he considered them, with a new approach to language.[5] If language were reduced to simple building blocks, it could be rebuilt step by step in ways that would avoid misunderstanding and superstition; language would be in the service of science at last. Carnap had studied Leibniz, the seventeenth-century philosopher who had tried to construct a logical language, and concluded that the time was right to take another stab at a similar project.

When I returned home for Christmas, I used these new intellectual tools to attack religion. My father and I were sitting in our living room, in deep armchairs that had sheepskins thrown over them to preserve the leather, surrounded by bookshelves my father had built himself to save money. He had returned to the Catholic Church after a period of rebellion during his time in the commune and now he was slightly irritated by my radical pronouncements, though he tried to answer them with good humor. I felt he was being evasive and, channeling Carnap, I declared, "There is no referent for the word God." I added: "It is not a well-formed term. It shouldn't be allowed in the language." "Well," my father replied, "languages don't work according to such simple ideas." "My ideas aren't simple!" I shot back. "They are logical." My father responded with something that I remember sounding like *"mada kacao tilis."* Very likely, it was another one of his mock imitations of Esperanto. I got up and left in a huff, banging the door.

Neither my father, nor I, knew at the time that Carnap was a passionate promoter of Esperanto.[6] My father wasn't a student of languages the way I was, but somehow, instinctively, he had come up with the perfect reply.

I now wish I hadn't stormed out that night because I realize that my father with his made-up Esperanto and I with my Carnap logic were much closer than we thought. While ostensibly quarreling about religion, we were really grappling with language and the question of whether languages can ever be constructed artificially. We just couldn't make ourselves understood.

As if the unexpected connection between Carnap and Esperanto wasn't enough, I also found that Carnap's intellectual father, Leibniz, had come across Rotwelsch. Leibniz knew how difficult it would be to establish his logical language, and apparently, he started to look for successful models. This must have been how he heard about Rotwelsch, which was widely regarded as a made-up language, an artificial creation that had unexpectedly taken off among thieves.[7] Leibniz wanted to make it clear that his logical language had nothing to do with the artificial cant of beggars, but that he mentioned it at all betrayed that he saw an affinity. (I also found that Leibniz developed a theory of names very close to my grandfather's, in that he thought names encapsulated an entire history and that by studying a name, you could learn everything about its bearer.)

More and more, it seemed to me that Rotwelsch was haunting language philosophy, mocking the attempts of linguists and philosophers to create artificial languages. Or was it I who was haunted by Rotwelsch and who kept seeing everything through its lens? One thing was certain: there was no better way to study language philosophy than through Rotwelsch. Leibniz, Zamenhof, and Carnap spent their lives trying to create new languages, as if forever playing at pig Latin.

All this talk of artificial, constructed languages made me realize that I hadn't thought enough about so-called natural—normal—languages. Our first language is baby talk, the undifferentiated babble of a toddler. Surely this was the most natural of all languages, though not quite a language in the traditional sense. Then comes our second language, the sounds we learn to form during the first years of our lives, what is conventionally called a mother tongue. Learning a mother tongue (or several mother tongues, or indeed father tongues) is subtractive: it's actually about unlearning things, about leaving out sounds. Babies speaking baby talk make sounds that span a wide spectrum, but then they learn to cut out more and more, and what remains are the limited but distinctive sounds of a language they have picked up from adults.

And then, as soon as children have learned one or several languages, they invent their own. Children love the idea of a secret or constructed language, with pig Latin being only one among many. Even when kids and teenagers don't actually go to the trouble of learning a secret language, they develop expressions and terms that adults don't get. Learning languages and constructing special ones for particular groups seem to go hand in hand.

The thieves' language closest to pig Latin comes from London's East End, so-called Cockney rhyming slang. It is based on common word pairings such as apples and pears. The second of those terms is then rhymed with a third term that is vaguely associated with it, in this case stairs, because fruit stalls used to stack fruit and vegetables in "stairs." Now "apple and pairs" is used to mean stairs. Another example is bees and honey, which is rhymed with money.

When I compared Rotwelsch with constructed languages such as Esperanto, the logical languages of Leibniz and Carnap, or even to pig Latin or Cockney rhyming slang, I was struck by how different Rotwelsch felt, much more like an actual, living language. There was very little that was constructed or artificial about it. Many of the claims about this language, that it was an artificial creation like a secret code, were extremely doubtful. If Rotwelsch was the secret language of robbers, wouldn't speaking Rotwelsch automatically identify you as a criminal?

Wouldn't criminal parents beat their children into *not* speaking Rotwelsch to keep their identity hidden? Speaking Rotwelsch surely attracted unwanted attention.

The Rotwelsch archive needed to be read against the grain, against its built-in bias, more rigorously than I had understood. Once one discounted the bias, the archive showed something typical of members of an underclass or a distinct sociological group: code-switching. When in the presence of others, especially middle-class citizens or the police, Rotwelsch speakers would avoid using this language, and switch into the in-group code only when left alone. This is how sociolects work, as the glue that holds a community together.

ROTWELSCH LESSON:

A GREETING FOR ALIENS TO BE INCLUDED

IN FUTURE SPACE MISSIONS

Welschlings, wir wähnen heissen in eisen und kohl mit gent der eifer martine, grandig olm.
[Dear Aliens, we want to live in peaceful community with the peoples of the earthen lands, and of the great world.]

Other Terms Useful for Communicating with Aliens

Dibbert ihr Rotwelsch? = Do you speak Rotwelsch?
Seit ihr kochemer? = Are you in the know?
Wähnen baffern bomditerr? = Would you like to eat some potatoes?
Zi sanctus? = Or some hard liquor?
Wir ratzen in a prudenz. = Let's go to a dive bar.

Chapter 10

THE STORY OF AN ARCHIVIST

———

While following these various paths to understanding my family's relation to Rotwelsch, I kept trying to imagine how my grandfather must have felt as he watched his older son devote himself to the thieves' language that he himself had tried to eliminate. Could my grandfather keep his mouth shut about his own opinions on the subject? Did he sense that his son was punishing him by working on Rotwelsch? Contemplating this strange relationship, I decided it was time for me to dig deeper into my grandfather's past. When and how did he get involved in Nazi ideology? After my father and his brother had found out that he had been entangled with the Nazis, they'd asked the same questions and received few answers. All they had were two objects: my father had the picture with the swastika; and my uncle had his father's copy of *Mein Kampf.* What did these two mementos add up to?

There was one place where I could find out more, a place I had been avoiding, perhaps because I was afraid of what I would discover there: the Bavarian State Archive. After the war, my grandfather had been able to resume his old profession as an archivist and had worked there until his retirement in the 1970s. I wrote to the Bavarian State Archive asking whether they had information on their former employee Karl Puchner. A librarian informed me that of course they had an entire file on Professor Dr. Karl Puchner, correcting my omission of these titles, since he had been the archive's director. Perhaps it should have been obvious to me. My grandfather had been an archivist, after all, and archivists keep files, even on themselves.

All through my research into Rotwelsch—and my family— I had come to appreciate the power of archives, from police archives to my uncle's personal archive, their power but also their bias. Archives decide what to preserve and how to preserve it; they set the record and relish that power. I was about to approach the archive in which the state kept its most official documents, and I was apprehensive about what I might find.

Next time I was in Munich, I went to the state archives, which were kept close to where Hitler had staged his putsch and not far from my father's and uncle's commune. The building was a grand nineteenth-century structure, designed to inspire confidence and awe. In front of it stood a statue of a horse without a rider.

To access the records stored there, I went through elaborate vetting procedures, seemingly designed to intimidate. But I kept telling myself that I had a right to be there, not only as the descendant of a former director but also as someone who was doing an investigation into the history of the institution. What business did a former Nazi sympathizer have overseeing the records of the German past? I was researching not only the history of my grandfather but also the history of the archive.

Eventually, after I had filled out several forms, obtained an ID, submitted a request, and waited, a low-level clerk of the type that seems to exist only in archives slowly approached, hunched over a wheeled cart. On it was a towering pile of papers: my grandfather's file.[1] It was much larger than I had expected at hundreds of pages long. I stacked the pile on my table and delicately picked up the first page, briefly wondering whether I should be wearing gloves or at least wash my hands. I turned around to ask the clerk, but he had already shuffled off. I looked around at the half dozen other users of the archive, but, absorbed in their own documents they paid me no heed, and I decided to proceed bare-handed.

As I gingerly turned the pages over, careful not to break off edges of the brittle paper, the story of my grandfather's professional life slowly emerged. The file contained plenty of bureaucratic information about his career, including documents concerning minor squabbles and complaints. In one, he and a colleague fought over the employee-owned vegetable garden. Each as recalcitrant as the other, they had taken their disagreement to the director of the State Archive, who settled the matter in good humor. My grandfather was given a strawberry bed and the use of an apple tree as well as a pear tree. He seemed content with this decision; there was no further mention of the affair in the file.

I enjoyed the deep dive into a past when archives owned vegetable gardens over which young archivists could squabble. I also enjoyed the odd way his superiors evaluated my grandfather. One official assessment singles out his "positive appearance" and notes that he "makes a good impression," is a "hard worker," "energetic," and "seeks to improve himself."[2] This was not how I remembered him, but a photo from the period shows a sleek, presentable young professional.

Appearance was not everything. His superiors also noted that his greatest talent, for an archivist, was as a writer. Karl Puchner, the son of a low-level business clerk, was poised for a good career.

The next batch of documents revealed another reason that Karl Puchner was favored by his superiors. It included a form,

printed on cheap paper, on which my grandfather let it be known that he had joined the Nationalist Socialist Party. His membership number was 267,450 and the year, 1930.

Despite everything I had learned, despite his articles against Jews and Rotwelsch speakers, I was unprepared for this revelation. I had presumed—or, in any case, hoped—that he'd joined, as so many people had, for careerist reasons later on in the Nazi years, once it was clear which way the wind was blowing, around the time he had published his hateful article, in 1934. But now I found that he had joined the party early, three years before Hitler's rise to power, at a time when few people would have predicted that the Nazis would prevail. I had to conclude that he'd joined because he'd been a true believer.

Where had his political convictions come from? I looked into his early career at the University of Munich. His dissertation advisor was an apolitical, old-school historian, but I noticed that Karl also thanked Karl Alexander von Müller, for whom he later worked on a research project.[3] Von Müller had been one of the first German Rhodes scholars sent to Oxford, an experience that seems to have done little to thwart his future career as a Nazi historian. He was especially valuable to the Nazis since he came from an old and widely respected conservative family. Several of the early Nazis, including Hermann Göring, Rudolf Hess, and Baldur von Schirach attended von Müller's lectures, as did Adolf Hitler. Thrilled by this audience, which was not yet powerful but politically on the move, von Müller became an avid supporter of Hitler, proud to be seen as a teacher of these rabble-rousing politicians. He even defended Hitler after Hitler's putsch failed. When the Nazis assumed power, von Müller knew that his time had come. He "cleansed" the university of Jewish professors, and after he became head of the Bavarian

Academy had the distinct pleasure of forcing out Albert Einstein. Unlike his student Karl Puchner, however, von Müller never attacked Jews in print. He was too old-school to stoop that low.

It was at this moment in my investigation that I found a copy of a request from Karl to deliver a lecture for a Nazi educational organization called Strength Through Joy in 1934. As a topic, he proposed family names as racial markers. Permission for his lecture was granted.

I continued to read about Karl Puchner's career, skimming requests for reimbursements and minor promotions, when I came across information that gave me an even bigger shock: my grandfather had joined the SA. Hitler had founded this organization in the 1920s, putatively to provide "protection" for his followers during rallies, which often led to violent clashes with Communists. Members of the SA were colloquially known as Brown Shirts because of their brown uniforms. My grandfather donned the brown uniform on January 9, 1933, a few weeks before Hitler was sworn in as chancellor.

By 1933, the SA had become an all-purpose paramilitary organization, used not only to attack protesters but also to organize boycotts of Jewish businesses and to intimidate Jews, Roma, and other undesirables. The SA did the dirty work for the Nazi Party, and in 1933 they were poised to become an important organization, perhaps even more influential than the German army, which was seen as insufficiently aligned with the party. The SA had its own ranks, and my grandfather rose to *Sturmmann* (storm man), one rung above the simple *Mann* (man).

For his induction into the SA, my grandfather had to present the so-called expanded proof of ancestry, tracing his

Aryan provenance back three generations, not the two generations required of the general population. For my grandfather, this was child's play. Tracing histories of names and producing genealogies was his profession. He could have gone back further, all the way to Hans Martin Puchner, the distant ancestor who had left his wife and children to become a traveling musician, if necessary.

Karl Puchner's political engagement served him well. On October 10, 1934, he received a temporary position at the archive and swore the following oath: "I swear that I will follow the Führer of the German Reich, Adolf Hitler, with loyalty and obedience, so help me God."[4] He must have been pleased: four years after entering the party, and almost two years after becoming a Storm Trooper, his future was secured.

There was one problem with Karl Puchner's career as a Nazi. The meteoric rise of the SA began to worry other organizations within the Nazi state, including the army and the Schutzstaffel, or SS, then still a minor paramilitary organization. Hitler, who liked to play his minions off against one another, decided to promote the SS over the SA, and eventually weakened the SA permanently. In what came to be known as the Night of the Long Knives, he had the leader of the SA, Ernst Röhm, arrested and executed, after denouncing him as a homosexual (his sexual orientation had been well-known in Nazi circles and had not been a problem until then). The organization continued to exist, but its importance was much diminished. Its last moment of fame came in 1938 during Kristallnacht, a large-scale attack on businesses owned by Jews, in which Storm Troopers smashed storefronts and arrested tens of thousands of Jews and sent them to concentration camps.

As I read about my grandfather's Nazi career, I tried to

imagine what he had done. By 1938, he was no longer an active SA trooper. He had left the SA in 1936, no doubt sensing that it no longer served his purposes. Instead, he became more involved with the party, working as party representative for a small neighborhood. In this position, he was supposed to monitor people's dedication to the party, report on any suspicious behavior, and, of course, denounce any Jews who might be hiding. Among his chief duties was compiling files on his neighbors, something he was well equipped to do. I didn't find any evidence that he actually engaged in these activities, but whatever files he compiled would have been long lost.

His superiors were pleased with Karl's academic and political activities. One notes in an internal file: "Karl has belonged to the NSDAP since 1930 and has distinguished himself as a Nazi fighter. He was a member of the SA from 1933–1936. . . . He is one of the great hopes of future leadership."[5] Another spells out that Karl's early party membership proves the sincerity of his political convictions, declaring that Karl has placed his work "in the service of the Nazi State" and singling him out as a "born leader." Another promotion identifies him as an "early party member," the badge of honor of having joined before the party had become powerful. (After the Nazi Party was voted into power, so many people wanted to join that the party periodically closed down the application process.)

The file revealed occasions when Karl used his Nazi connections to good effect. He'd been working in a provincial archive but wanted to return to Munich. I found a request for leave to meet with a highly placed party representative, a *Gauleiter*, in another town, on January 18, 1939. He gives no reason, and the *Gauleiter* has nothing to do with archival work. Miraculously, a few months later, his dream came true and he was called back to Munich.

Before my grandfather could begin the coveted job, Hitler invaded Poland, which meant that my grandfather was drafted into the army. He was sent to the western front, wounded, and spent most of his time during the rest of the war as an archivist in occupied Netherlands. It sounded like a nice, safe desk job. But what exactly did he do there? Was he trying to separate true Dutch names from deceptively camouflaged ones? Was he helping round up people with suspicious names? He received a medal, the Kriegsverdienstkreuz, second class, the second-highest medal for someone not serving on the front, reserved for those who were doing crucial work in the occupied territories, including members of the security service who shot civilians and Jews. The medal was presented to Karl by Arthur Seyß-Inquart, a particularly rabid Nazi who sent 100,000 Jews to concentration camps and who, when the war was lost, threat-

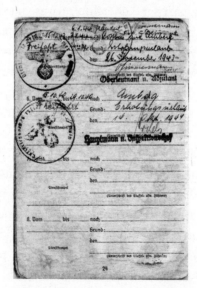

ened to destroy all levees to flood the Netherlands. He was among the few to be convicted at the Nuremberg trials and executed.

I lost sight of Karl's whereabouts in the last months of the war. His military pass ends in October 1944; after that, there's no trace of him.

The only information I could obtain was of a more personal nature: he returned to Munich with a Dutch girlfriend, leaving my grandmother with her children in the countryside. Karl was yet another Puchner who had done a rabbit on his family.

=====

The next sighting of Karl Puchner was in June 1945, a month after German capitulation, when he reported for duty at his last place of work, the State Archive in the provincial town of Amberg. It was here that he was spotted by the Military Government of the U.S. Army (the same army that liberated my maternal great-grandfather). All the activities that had served him so well for the past fifteen years were now poison: the early party membership; the SA membership; his work as party functionary. Karl was dismissed from the job and accused of being a willing collaborator.

I don't know where he lived then, or how. Were he and his Dutch girlfriend shacked up in some half-bombed-out apartment in the ruins of the city? For a period, he was drafted into an improvised service to collect firewood, but he was dismissed because of his war wounds and instead started to work for the State Archive in Munich. He was now working for free, no doubt hoping to get in through the back door.

His main problem, apart from avoiding starvation, was the

de-Nazification process. He was classified not as a mere "fellow traveler" but as someone who was "implicated" in the atrocities of the Nazi regime. How could he wiggle out of this classification?

The next section of the file, which recorded his dealings with the U.S. authorities, made for fascinating reading. Karl's first line of defense was typical: he was never a true believer. Karl claimed that he entered the party out of "youthful inexperience" and "naïve trust in the Führer, who disappointed me, like millions of other Germans." For his SA membership, he blamed the former director of the archive, Dr. Riedner. "He demanded that I join the SA, and his demand was like a command," Karl wrote.[6] There was nothing he could do, he had to obey, much as he wished to avoid it. The best thing about this line of defense was that Dr. Riedner was unable to either substantiate or contradict this claim, because Dr. Riedner was dead.

What about his work for the party? Karl claimed that he had never worked for the Nazis, that he didn't like it, and also that he couldn't have refused this work because refusal could have cost him his job, or worse. Finally, as proof of his inner opposition to the Nazi Party and the SA, he reminded his interrogators that he had sent his two sons, my father and my uncle, to a Catholic kindergarten and not to the Nazi kindergarten. I am not sure how impressed his interrogators were by this act of resistance.

Karl had one more trick up his sleeve. He claimed that his low party number, which signified early party membership, was a clerical error; in truth, he had become a party member only in 1933. I had some difficulties piecing together what actually happened, but in the end the archival record was clear. In 1930, my grandfather had become a party member in a section that was later dissolved, which meant that technically he had to reapply for membership in 1933. He had kept that later membership application and could now present it as if it were his only one, claiming that the earlier form was some sort of record created by the party because he had participated in a party event without actually joining. There is no doubt that he had become a member in 1930. He had boasted about it throughout the Nazi years, and his superiors had mentioned it every time he had been promoted.

Initially, the trick didn't quite work. Someone at a ministry had seen the Nazi forms on which the early party membership was proudly presented and in which Karl's superiors had praised him as a reliable "fighter" for the Nazi cause. Karl panicked and found more people, including someone he described as a "political exile," to serve as character witnesses. It was a war fought with forms and files, the type of war Karl was good at.

History came to his aid. By 1948, the Cold War had erupted and the priorities of the U.S. occupation had shifted from punishing those, like my grandfather, who were implicated in the Nazi regime to turning the western part of Germany into an ally against communism. Despite the objections of the Bavarian Ministry of Education, my grandfather's version of events—that he had joined the party in 1933 out of youthful naïveté, while holding on to his Catholic faith to the disapproval of his Nazi superiors (as evidenced by his unwavering support for Catholic kindergartens)—prevailed. On May 11, 1948, he was classified as nothing but a fellow traveler, fined six hundred *marks*, and let go.

His struggles to rehabilitate himself weren't entirely over, but he had navigated the biggest obstacle. The remaining problem was that work at the archive was a government position, and for

civil servants the criteria for the hiring and promotion of politically implicated persons were higher than for other employees.
Another paper war started, and it would take a few years for my
grandfather to prevail. His superiors helped him, writing to the
ministry again and again, praising his abilities, downplaying his
political history. Finally, they argued that giving Karl Puchner a proper job would "contribute to maintaining the internal
peace." It sounded almost like a threat. If you don't give the former Nazis their jobs back, there will be a civil war.

Ultimately they succeeded, probably not because of these
empty threats but because of exhaustion and willed oblivion.
In 1949, Karl Puchner returned to his old job, and in 1951 he
became a civil servant, which meant job security and a nice
pension, for life. The path was clear for him to rise through
the ranks, and less than a decade later, he was director of the
archive and enjoyed a teaching position at the university, one of
the chief archivists in the land.

It is difficult to say what his personal life was like during this
time. My father once told me that my grandmother, Karl's wife,
had my father and his brother call their father on the phone
throughout these years, pleading with him to come back to the
family. In the late forties he did. Perhaps he wanted to bring
the period of disorder to an end. Perhaps he felt that living
apart from his family would be bad for his career. I don't know
whether the Dutch girlfriend had been with him the whole time
in between. Had she been a collaborator in the Netherlands
and therefore forced to flee, an accomplice to my grandfather's
attempts to weasel his way out of culpability?

No one knows. Karl Puchner didn't dwell on the past. He
didn't talk about his fifteen years as a Nazi or his three years as
a political suspect. Instead, he returned to his family and to his

old subject, the history of names. He published several books on arcane archival materials and humbly described his work as a mere auxiliary to the work of historians, implying that all archivists did was tend documents, which historians then used, interpreted, and turned into historical narratives.

The question of why my grandfather joined the Nazis and how he viewed the remaining years of his life was something the archive was silent about, as was Karl himself. Karl's Nazi superiors had singled out discretion as one of his outstanding qualities. Karl Puchner could keep a secret, and this is what he did for the rest of his life, the only interruption being the moment when my father saw him wearing a swastika in a photograph. Karl weathered this storm of outrage, as he had weathered all the others. He was able to reestablish good relations with his family despite his Nazi past and despite having left them after the war in what was surely the most difficult time of their lives. In his obituaries, he was praised as a historian of names, as the director of the Bavarian State Archive, and as a university teacher.

===

As I contemplated his life emerging from the hundreds of pages in that stack of documents, I was struck by a paradox: Karl Puchner profited from postwar oblivion and silence, but all documents that demonstrate his Nazi past and his lies to the U.S. authorities were right here, in front of me. They had been here all along. His two sons could have taken an easy stroll from their commune down to the archive and had a look. His file was a time bomb that could have gone off at any moment.

Karl Puchner must have been aware of his personnel file. It

was, after all, in his own archive, the archive over which he presided and over which he had complete authority. It would have been easy for him to sneak in and eliminate the evidence of his early party membership and of the way he lied his way out of de-Nazification. But he didn't do that.

On the contrary, he tended his own file lovingly to the end. One of the last entries is from 1975, long after his retirement. He is writing to his old archive to let the staff know that he has just been named an honorary member of the International Committee for the Study of Names. He requests that this item be added to his personnel file so that the file is up-to-date and complete. It was a shocking document for me because it confirmed that my grandfather knew the contents of his file, that he was always thinking about it, even in retirement, that he wanted this latest news to be there and the file to be complete.

While much of what is inside the file is bad, the very existence of the file, the fact that my grandfather preserved it despite of what it contained, says something else: my grandfather was a dedicated archivist. He believed that files must be preserved no matter what. If there is anything good about his file, anything redemptive, it's the fact that he didn't destroy it and instead tended it even beyond his retirement, an archivist to the end.

When I went back to the archive the next day to look over some documents again, I noticed a new entry: my own request to view the archive. It, too, is now part of my grandfather's official file. Perhaps the file wasn't really complete until that moment.

For me, the most devastating document in my grandfather's file is one that comes early on, from 1934, a note from a supervisor congratulating my grandfather on his marriage to my grandmother. It is written in a somewhat convoluted, pedantic manner, but also takes an odd flight of fancy, riffing on the work of the archivist and the nature of the archive:

Dear Colleague: On the occasion of your marriage, I wish you and your bride great happiness from the bottom of my heart.

For an archivist, marriage is especially important because it is sealed with a document that constitutes the foundation of a building—an archive—that otherwise would only be of professional interest to him. This marriage certificate is soon joined by bills from landlords, tailors, and butchers, and then, God willing, by certificates of baptisms, vaccinations, and school transcripts or, on the other hand, by promotion and transfer documents. Be warned that not everything that will be preserved in this archive will be pleasant, but I dearly hope that the greater part of this future archive of your life will speak not of pain and suffering, but of pleasure and happiness.[7]

The note is prescient: my grandfather's file, the archive of his life, really does capture much about him. Unfortunately, the good wishes of his supervisor that most of this archive tell a story of pleasure and happiness, not of pain and suffering, were not fulfilled.

In my research, I have come across many archives, from the Rotwelsch records kept by generations of policemen to Joseph Kresser's trial documents, and now my grandfather's own state archive. These archives speak the cold language of bureaucracy that can feel inhuman, uninterested in personal stories. But I have come to respect official documents and those who keep them, perhaps because I am a descendant of archivists, of people who dedicate their lives to guarding their archives through changing political times, telling stories of good and ill, stories that keep changing with the times. Even my uncle's Rotwelsch archive wasn't all that different. For all his rebellion, he dedicated his life to the same type of job as his father had.

As I was contemplating my grandfather's personnel file, I kept thinking about secrets. Was a secret simply something that was hidden? Not necessarily. It was rather something waiting to be found: a button on your father's vest in an old photograph; a *zinken* carved into a tree or discreetly painted on the side of a house; a file in an archive, carefully preserved.

ROTWELSCH WORDS FOR NAZIS

Aschkunesische Martine = the land of the Ashkenas (German-speaking Jews; here it means Germany)

Gabeln = to swear; literally, fork, because the raised hand in an oath looks like the shape of a fork

Humpeln = to limp; can also mean to go or to follow

Baldower = scout in robbery; can also mean leader

Nit kochem = not cunning (there is no Rotwelsch word for obedience)

Keilerplatte = gang of criminals (from Romani)

Chapter 11

JUDGMENT AT HIKELS-MOKUM

I had left Nuremberg for college and never returned, and the longer I lived in America, the more distant the city of my birth became. But I could never entirely forget it. Whenever I told people that I had grown up in Nuremberg, there was a quick pause, followed by an "Oh. . . ." I could imagine the images that were flashing through my interlocutors' minds, images of rallies and of Nazi flags. Somehow, I had been born into the epicenter of Nazism; it was part of the patina of shame that colored my life abroad.

Growing up, I had known Nuremberg as a city whose past overshadowed its present. It had been an important city during the Middle Ages, its labyrinthine streets, several city walls and a towering castle reminding me every day of its glorious past. I had served as an altar boy in one of the city's large, architecturally significant gothic cathedrals. Nuremberg had also been an important center for the Reformation, a printing hub that spread Luther's words across Germany.

From my uncle, I knew another view of the city, that of Rot-welsch speakers, who called it Hikels-Mokum. *Mokem* meant place in Yiddish; *Hikels* came from the Yiddish *heykhl*, for palace or temple, but could also mean court. Nuremberg was the seat of the regional power—the court city. This Rotwelsch name was prescient, for this was what Nuremberg would become: the city of the trial, the place where Germany was judged.

I was also aware of the notoriety my hometown had acquired internationally. I vaguely knew that the city's medieval flair had caught the imagination of Adolf Hitler, who selected it as the venue for his annual party rallies. Party members in different regional divisions, as well as the SA and the SS, would march three miles from the city center to the open-air rally grounds, which were lined with huge stone stalls, one of which included a platform from which Hitler would speak. Using a flag from the First World War, a so-called blood flag, or *Blutfahne*, Hit-ler would ritually touch the flags of these marching SA and SS troops to signal that he was going to take revenge for the humiliating defeat Germany had suffered in that war.

My own mental images of these rallies were shaped by the movie *Triumph of the Will* by Leni Riefenstahl, Hitler's favorite filmmaker. Along with other Nazi propaganda and *Mein Kampf*, the film was forbidden in postwar Germany, but it could be shown for pedagogical purposes as long as it was introduced and framed by a historian. This was how I saw it at a local cin-ema when I was in my teens.

The historian warned about the film's content, but also said that Riefenstahl's innovative cinematography had earned it a place in film history. Heavily staged, the film used the 1934 rally as its material, reveling in its organized crowds march-ing by the monumental stone stage. Hitler had held his first rally here in 1933, the year he attained power; 1934 was the year when Riefenstahl shot her film; and in 1935, Hitler used the party rally to proclaim the Racial Laws, with their precise definition of who was a Jew and who wasn't. This was why they were known as the Nuremberg Laws, heaping more shame on my hometown. The 1938 rally was the last, since a gathering of all Nazi leaders was deemed too dangerous after the outbreak of World War II.

Triumph of the Will is also a celebration of Nuremberg. Before moving to the rally grounds with their huge geometric moments and marching masses, it lingers in the old city. The film ends there as well, with Hitler standing in front of the same gothic church in which I had served as an altar boy. Watching my hometown through the eyes of Riefenstahl's cameras was an odd experience, presenting the Nazi view of the city. This, I realized, was how the world viewed the place where I grew up.

When I watch Riefenstahl's film now, I wonder whether my grandfather, that early party member and SA *Sturmmann*, was in the crowd she was filming. He had grown up in Nuremberg, his parents lived there, and he worked in a nearby town. Might not the party, or the SA, have sent this dedicated Nazi, who made a good impression and had exhibited such compelling leadership qualities, to visit his hometown and to hail the Führer? Did he even make an annual ritual of it? If Karl attended the 1934 rally, he would have witnessed Hitler's attempt to patch over his recent crackdown on the SA. Prominently and publicly, Hitler confirmed his commitment to his Storm Troopers: "If someone sins against the spirit of my SA, it does not affect the SA, only the person who has sinned."

If my grandfather attended the rally, or saw the film, he would have felt even more gratified toward the end, when the film moved to a large tent where Hitler addressed a smaller crowd of party stalwarts: "All decent Germans are National Socialists. But only the best Germans are party members," echoing an early moment when he acknowledged that "old fighters might have been looking back with nostalgia to the days when it was difficult to be a National Socialist."

I was familiar with the rally grounds long before I saw Riefenstahl's film. They were mostly abandoned, though occasionally the large stalls were used for Formula One car races. The local soccer club rented an adjacent field for practice. A large coliseum-like structure, whose interior courtyard was meant to be covered by a dome that was never built, was where the city brought towed cars. The city knew that it had to remember the role it played in National Socialism, but it didn't know what to do with its abandoned monuments, so charged with history that they couldn't be torn down or committed to some other, permanent use.

The arena had been built to last a thousand years—the Nazis thought their reign would last that long. They had even anticipated what would come afterward. Hitler liked to think in world-historical terms, and as an aspiring art and architecture student, he had adored half-destroyed remnants of ancient civilizations. He wanted his own buildings to look as good as ruins once the thousand years were up. There was even a word for it, *Ruinenwert* (literally, ruin-value), which rated a building according to how good it would look as a ruin. The abandoned rally grounds were meant to look the way they did now, minus the car races and the parking lots. They were only ahead of schedule by about 950 years.

These Nazi party grounds became part of the standard tour of the city I would give to visitors: here, on your right is the imposing castle, towering over the medieval city center; on your left are the beautiful gothic cathedrals; and over there you see the grounds where Herr Hitler held his annual rallies and declared the racial laws. The juxtapositions were uncomfortable, but they suggested a line that extended from Germany's medieval life and Martin Luther to Adolf Hitler. The two eras, captured in the monuments of my city, were connected.

While the grounds of the Nuremberg rallies were a place I had visited many times, the grounds of the Nuremberg trials were not. I remembered no signs or exhibitions about them growing up. Schools, at least my school, didn't go there. I didn't even know which building they had taken place in. That Nuremberg had given its name not only to the Nuremberg Laws but also to the international tribunal that had judged them was not something the city chose to commemorate.

When I returned to Nuremberg a few years ago, I learned that the trials had been held in the Palace of Justice, which was still used as the main courthouse. I wasn't allowed to enter, since the hall where the trial had been held, much smaller than it had seemed in the pictures, was currently in use. An exhibition about the Nuremberg trials had opened recently, in 2016, and there were plans to decommission the hall and turn it into a museum.

Nuremberg was chosen as the place for putting the Nazi regime on trial not primarily because of the party rallies but because this court building had survived American carpet-bombing and was conveniently connected to a functioning prison in which Nazi leaders could be held. In the immediate postwar period, when the victors divided Germany up into occupation zones, the city was also considered a good choice because it fell within the American sector, and the trials were overseen logistically by the Americans. But in addition to these practical considerations, the city must have struck many as an appropriate place to bring the Nazi regime to trial.

The Allied forces, eager to show that the trials were not a case of victors' justice, gave the defendants legal representation. Inevitably, there were grumblings that the defense had fewer resources to research and marshal evidence than the prosecution. Some also worried that the trial was conducted according to an Anglo-American system that was not well-known to the accused, their counsel, and the German population.

Despite complaints about the process, the real goal of these trials wasn't legal but historical. The Nazi regime had visited such horror upon the world that it needed to be judged by the world. To address the scale of it, a new legal category was invented: crimes against humanity. The new category was suspect from a legal point of view since it meant that a new law was applied retroactively, something that is illicit in almost all legal traditions. But in this case, it was fitting: since the Nazis had invented a regime of unprecedented cruelty, the terms of their indictment were also unprecedented.

One of the biggest challenges faced by the Nuremberg trials was the sheer number of languages spoken by victims, including Polish, Czech, Hungarian, and Yiddish. Witnesses who had survived the camps described their experience in the language of the camps, the Babel of languages described by Primo Levi. There was the extra difficulty of capturing life in concentration camps in all its unvarnished horror. For this purpose, translators who themselves had been incarcerated were hired, despite the strain it put on them to relive their recent experiences.

Finally, there was the peculiar German spoken by the Nazis.

My guide to this language was Victor Klemperer.[1] He came from a Jewish family, but had converted to Protestantism and married a woman the Nazis considered "Aryan." Initially, he had been able to hold on to his job teaching Romance languages and literatures at the Technical University of Dresden even when the campaign against "Jews" was already under way (throughout, Klemperer refused the label imposed on him by the Nazis). It started with petty chicaneries. One day, Klemperer was no longer allowed to sit on park benches; the next, he was required to go shopping only during certain times. A bigger blow for him was when he was forbidden from using the library. Then he was fired from his job, forced to leave his home, and sent to work in a factory, where he was not allowed to eat or communicate with non-Jewish workers (some of whom broke these rules and talked to him nonetheless). If the war had not ended in May 1945, or soon thereafter, he would likely not have survived.

His diary is a unique document in that it records the repressive conditions during the Third Reich through the lens of language, what Klemperer regarded as the Nazis' corruption of German. The Nazis didn't construct an entirely new language; instead they twisted existing terms.[2]

Most obvious was the vocabulary of race, of Germans against Jews, the *Volksgemeinschaft* (community of the people) versus all foreigners. More remarkable for Klemperer was the fact that the Nazis changed the meaning of ordinary words or gave them new values. One example was "fanatic," which had never been used positively before. In a stunning and perverse feat, the Nazis turned this word into a positive one, inducing people to utter such sentences as in "I am a fanatic German" or "I am a fanatic hater of Jews." Being a fanatic was suddenly good.

The Nazis also borrowed from Christianity, especially

Catholicism, despite their campaign against it. Klemperer noted the rituals conducted at Nuremberg involving the "blood flag," and he found similar borrowings in their language. The Nazis demanded "belief" everywhere, above all in their policies. To this end, they changed the Christian notion of belief by modifying it with the adjective "blind," demanding "blind belief" in the Führer. *Führer* was another term they gave a new twist. Traditionally, it had been used in all kinds of benign contexts, including for city guides (*Stadtführer*), but now *Führer* meant only one thing: Adolf Hitler. Klemperer also noted the preponderance of superlatives such as "eternal," "gigantic," "grand," and "huge."

Nazi language was designed to discourage pause and reflection. It favored terms such as "spontaneous," "will," and "action." Klemperer detected a similar tendency in details such as punctuation marks. Instead of question marks or semicolons, he found the Nazis favored exclamation marks, which would halt all thought processes by declaring the matter over! Klemperer called these various strategies *lingua Tertii Imperii*, Latin for the language of the Third Reich.

The flipside of this *lingua Tertii Imperii* was a cynical use of euphemisms, terms meant to hide the brutal reality of the regime. Klemperer called them "veiled terms." Deportations were termed "evacuations"; "special treatment" was a word for murder, and "enhanced interrogation" for torture. Even "concentration camp," a term borrowed from the Boer War in South Africa, was a euphemism because the Nazis had turned them into death camps. Veiled terms became more frequent as the war was not going well for the Nazis. Now military retreat was called "an adjustment" of the front; and the German "will" to fight was kept up by the promise of a so-called new weapon, or "miracle weapon," which never materialized.

Klemperer's notion of veiled terms reminded me of my grandfather's "camouflage names." Indeed, Klemperer had noticed the Nazi obsession with names, singling out their fixation on *echt* German names as well as a strange trend toward hyphenated first names (Karl-Dietrich, etc.). Names brought together racial identity and language and triggered the Nazi fear of language mixing, precisely what had driven my grandfather's own project.

Klemperer's diary describes how the Nazis' manipulation of language injected their thinking and their values into the way people spoke, even if they didn't think of themselves as being political in any particular way. Klemperer also noted that even in chastised postwar Germany, when the population was trying to return to democracy, the language of the Third Reich lingered on.

In order to dispense with the obfuscations of the *lingua Tertii Imperii* and to meet the other linguistic challenges, the Nuremberg trials turned to technology. The film *Judgment at Nuremberg*, through which the trials are now mostly remembered, captured this dimension quite neatly. Judges, prosecutors, witnesses, and defense lawyers all wear headphones. They constantly fiddle with them, get confused, and don't know how to use them. The Nuremberg trials were the place where simultaneous interpretation originated. Previously, translators would wait for a speech to be finished and then deliver the translated version. But because the Nuremberg trials were conducted in the three languages of the Allied forces, English, French, and Russian, plus the language of the defendants, waiting for each question and answer to be translated into three other languages would have dragged out the proceedings intolerably.

An American translator, Leon Dostert, working with technology provided by IBM, came up with a solution, a system which we now know so well: everyone was wired with microphones and headphones, a group of translators was separated by a glass wall, and listeners could use switches to choose their preferred language. For the cross-examination of witnesses, or interruptions by prosecutors and defense lawyers, who might speak different languages, several translators had to take turns at a moment's notice. *Judgment at Nuremberg* also shows another innovation that has endured until today: a flashing light with which a simultaneous interpreter could signal to a speaker to slow down. The technical setup, including six hundred headsets, required so many cables that the floor of the courtroom was covered with them.

Technology was only part of the challenge. Since simultaneous interpretation was brand-new, none of the translators had been trained in it, and they had to figure out how to do it on the fly. The stakes could not have been higher. The Nuremberg trials meant to indict those responsible for the most brutal regime in the history of mankind, and to do so before the eyes of the whole world. The result would very likely include death sentences, perhaps for most of the accused. Simultaneous interpretation was meant to provide seamless communication for the members of the tribunal but also for the defendants. Some defendants, including Hermann Göring, tried to use occasional problems with translation to complain about the unfairness of the proceedings. Other defendants, including Albert Speer, Hans Fritzsche, and Dr. Hjalmar Schacht, realized how crucial the system of simultaneous translation was for the workings of the trial and tried to ingratiate themselves with the translators. Of those three, none received death sentences, and two were acquitted, suggesting that those among

the accused who worked with, rather than against, the interpreters, who paused to help the translators and did not provoke
quarrels with them, were able to present their position in a
more positive light.

Despite the immense pressure, simultaneous interpretation
as pioneered in Nuremberg worked almost miraculously well.
Participants marveled that they could conduct seamless conversations with people whose language they didn't know. It was
almost as if Dostert had been inspired by the dream of universal
communication that had given rise to Esperanto but offered a
different solution: a heavily wired courtroom. The Babel of the
camps and the empty language of the Third Reich both were
heard at Nuremberg by all because they were translated with
unrelenting precision by teams of dedicated interpreters. Judgment at Nuremberg was also a judgment on language, on the
language the Nazis had used to commit their crimes.

After Nuremberg, simultaneous translation was introduced
to the United Nations, where a number of translators from
the Nuremberg trials went to work, and from there the sys-

tem spread all over the world. (Because the United Nations translates documents into many languages, its archives provide the material used by some of today's translation programs, including Google Translate, a belated linguistic triumph over a regime that had attacked the idea of universal communication.)

=

When my mother heard about my plan to visit the Nuremberg State Archive, where some of the trial documents would be housed, she was guarded. I could tell that she remembered my unpleasant discoveries about her husband's family and my unwanted corrections in her own family's stories about Joseph Kresser. Perhaps she was thinking: I wonder what he will dredge up this time.

Despite these worries, she reminded me that my great-uncle had worked there. We had had little contact with the family of Otto Puchner, Karl's brother, because of some quarrel I could never remember the details of, which meant that I had almost no recollection of Otto. Intrigued, I took the streetcar to the archive, another imposing building, conveniently located on Archive Street. On the application form, I declared that I had two objectives: the holdings of the Nuremberg trials; and the files of my great-uncle Otto Puchner.

At the reception desk, a young archivist chatted me up because I had indicated that I was also interested in Rotwelsch. He had heard of this secret language and wanted to know more. I gave him the three-minute version, and he told me that Otto had not only worked at the Nuremberg State Archive but had become the archive's director.[3] Due to a weak heart, he retired in 1975. Since I now knew all about personnel files, I requested his, but was told that I could look only at the parts that didn't mention anything about his children, who were still alive.

Examining the file, much smaller than my grandfather's (or had significant portions been withheld for privacy reasons?), it quickly became clear that Otto, seven years younger than Karl, had followed in his older brother's footsteps. He, too, had gone to university with the intention of becoming an archivist, and he had followed his older brother's political affiliations as well. On January 11, 1933, a few days after his brother, he joined the Brown Shirts, advanced to the position of *Sturmmann* in 1939, and remained an SA member until 1945. He didn't join the Nazi Party until May 1, 1937, which meant that his party number was embarrassingly high, 4,501,851, nothing like his brother's low six figures.

He had one advantage over his older brother: he knew how to pick the right dissertation advisor. While Karl had been stuck with an old-school historian, Otto chose the prominent Nazi historian of the period, von Müller, whom Karl had thanked in the acknowledgments of his dissertation and whom he undoubtedly recommended to his younger brother. Otto's dissertation from 1937 sounded extremely technical, and very much like his brother's: "The Geographic Names of the Dinkelsbühl District as Witness to German-Germanic Settlement" (Dinkelsbühl is a district near Nuremberg).[4]

Otto's career as an archivist was cut short by the war. He was less lucky than Karl, with his fine desk job. Otto fought in Poland and Russia and participated in the campaign on the eastern front in the winter of 1941–1942, for which the rapidly advancing army was badly equipped. His service earned him the Eastern Medal (Ostmedaille). After 1941 he was transferred to the western front, mostly to France, and he came through Belgium in 1944.

Otto's high party membership number made things much easier for him after the war than had been the case for his brother. Like Karl, Otto claimed that he had joined the SA out of pressure from his superiors and that his continuing practice as a Roman Catholic should be seen as proof that he had secretly rejected the Nazi worldview. He was lucky. As part of a limited amnesty declared in the winter of 1946–1947, he was classified as a mere fellow traveler and let go.

Once the de-Nazification process was behind him, Otto's challenge was how to rise in the archival service, where he had served only very briefly before the outbreak of the war. Soon an unexpected opportunity arose. His superiors were able to make a compelling argument about the need for more staff: the archive was being swamped with the files from the Nuremberg trials.

The argument prevailed, and Otto started to work in an informal position on the Nuremberg trial files in 1946. It was a growth area within the archive. More and more files came flooding in, both from the original trial and from the subsequent ones, such as the trial of the judges captured in *Judgment at Nuremberg*. Documents translated into four languages, along with sworn statements by the witnesses, amounted to 42 volumes of transcripts and associated documents plus an index volume, 5000 volumes in English, and 2500 volumes in German, French, and Russian: a total of 525,000 volumes.

The archive panicked. The director wrote to his superior asking for more people "because of the unprecedented volume of materials." He mentions, for 1946, 3208 numbered folders; for 1947, he can't even count in folders and instead counts them by the truckload, and none of which have yet been processed: "Not even the sworn statements from the first trial have been properly filed." Huffily, he reminds his superior that Otto Puch- ner had been working very hard at the archive, "carrying heavy books without being paid the supplement for manual labor"—a grave injustice.

In June 1947, Otto Puchner was sworn in as an official, full-time employee of the archive. He became a civil servant one year later (while his brother was still struggling with his de-Nazification process), and he landed a permanent job with lifetime tenure in 1950. The files give a clear reason for his rapid advancement: his "knowledgeable handling of the mate- rials pertaining to the Nuremberg trials." Otto Puchner, for- mer party member, SA *Sturmmann*, student of von Müller, had become, within a few years, "the number one expert" on the Nuremberg trials. As the volume of the documents from the Nuremberg trials grew, so Otto's fortunes grew as well, until he became the director of the archive in 1968. It was a bitter irony: a former Nazi was making a fine career in postwar Germany thanks to the Nuremberg trials, guarding the files on fellow students of von Müller—Hermann Göring, Baldur von Schi- rach, and Rudolf Hess—who had been among those accused and sentenced to death.

On my last day at the archive, an elderly employee, happy to meet the relative of a former director, showed me the large room in which all the files from the Nuremberg trials were kept. He proudly produced Hitler's last will and testament, which had been fixed on cardboard and put in a clear plastic cover, so it could be shown more easily, an item very much in demand. Just recently, he said, a film crew had requested it.

The document was short, three pages long. Hitler explained

that he had finally married his girlfriend Eva Braun, something he would have liked to have done earlier but felt it was incompatible with his service to the German *Volk*. His belongings should go to the party, and, should the party no longer exist, to the state. He devotes an equal amount of space to the disposition of his paintings, which he wishes to be housed in a museum in Linz, his birthplace. It's all pure Hitler, the grandiose ideas about *Volk* and state and party, the sentimental tone with respect to Eva Braun, the concern for his artistic bequest.

I poked around the archive, thinking of the simultaneous interpreters and clerks who had produced all these documents, of which copies are also held in The Hague and at the National Archives in Washington, D.C. I felt the dedication that spoke through the millions of files assembled here. This archival record, tended and organized by Otto Puchner, struck me as the thing Nuremberg should be most proud of. These vast holdings were a true monument to which schoolchildren should be sent by the busload: the record of Nuremberg as the place where the

concept of crimes against humanity had been pioneered, where an international court was assembled—and managed to communicate across several language barriers—demonstrating to the world the possibility of international justice.

The librarian showing me around wanted to chat about Otto Puchner, or rather, about his widow, who, after the death of Otto, had married Otto's successor, causing a bit of excitement, even scandal, in the otherwise staid halls of this old building. But I tried to get away as quickly as I could to ponder the two Puchner brothers, whose careers had been so eerily similar. I pictured them each guarding his own personnel file like the true archivists that they were. Did they ever speak about the past, about what they were preserving for the future? They died within a few months of each other in 1981.

══

A stone's throw from my great-uncle's archive is Nuremberg's beautiful old cemetery, where my father is buried. Among his papers, I found a poem from 1981, in which he stands before my grandfather's fresh grave.

> Grave,
> The grave of the father,
> at home in the cemetery,
> in the city of fathers
> where I often went looking
> for my father's image
> in vain, before it froze,
> when it was complete,
> ready to be remembered,

the pieces melded together to form a face,
incongruous pieces that wouldn't meld,
pieces that faced the other way and pieces
that went looking for themselves.
Father's face.

The father's face won't show itself, at least not fully, leaving much in the dark. Even though I have done my best to assemble as many pieces of information about my father's father as I could, I can't say that I've been able to make them fit any better than my father did.

My father's poem is what I think about when I stand by his grave for another reason as well: the phrase "city of fathers." Because this is how I think of Nuremberg now, the city of my father and his father, the Nazi city, and the court city: Hikels-Mokum.

ROTWELSCH LESSON:
NUREMBERG, BEFORE AND AFTER

German National Anthem
(Translated by my uncle into Rotwelsch)

Sachsolm, Sachsolm
über hackel,
über hackel in dem Zund,
wenn es alz voll Murr und Löwe
sepperisch zusammenstund,
von der Maas bis an die Memel,
von dem Belt bis an die Etsch,

Sachsolm, Sachsolm
über hackel,
über hack in dem Gequetsch.

Germany, Germany
above all,
above all in the world,
when, for protection and defense,
it always stands brotherly together,
from the Meuse to the Neman,
from the Adige to the Belt,
Germany, Germany
above all,
above all in the world.

Chapter 12

ERROR-SPANGLED BANNER

———

In 2007, I sang "The Star-Spangled Banner," all four strophes of it, for the first time. I had hummed it before, moving my lips as if I knew the lyrics, when it was played before sports events, but this time I had the lyrics in front to me. With me were two hundred people hailing from one hundred and twenty countries, tightly packed on a high floor of the Federal Building in downtown Manhattan. It is an ugly, institutional building; everything in it is cheaply made and has seen heavy use. Agents from the Department of Homeland Security had been herding us in one direction and our friends and families in another. Amanda, who had been looking forward to this event, wasn't used to being treated so dismissively and was slightly indignant. I, who had ample experience with high-handed immigration officials in several countries, tried my best to ignore them. Instead, I focused on the various badly photocopied sheets of paper that had been handed to us. They contained the Oath of Allegiance, the Pledge of Allegiance, and the lyrics of the American national anthem.

The Oath of Allegiance came first. I immediately liked the first sentence. "I hereby declare, under oath, that I absolutely, and entirely, renounce and abjure all allegiance and fidelity to any Foreign Prince, Potentate, State or Sovereignty of whom or of which I have heretofore been a subject or citizen." Who wouldn't be compelled by these old-fashioned phrases that conjured the eighteenth-century world of princes and potentates, all impressively capitalized? Even though the rest of the oath was clearly of a more recent vintage, with its talk of "national importance" and "noncombatant service," I felt the moral gravity of the language, almost against my instincts. I tended to be skeptical of patriotism, a reaction drilled into me by my postwar upbringing in Germany.

Next came the Pledge of Allegiance, which sounded much more modern throughout. I pledged allegiance "to the flag of the United States of America, and to the republic for which it stands, one nation, under god, indivisible, with liberty, and justice, for all" (the sheet of paper didn't capitalize "God" and added unnecessary commas around "and justice"). Flags were even worse for me than abstract patriotism: they reminded me of the scene in Leni Riefenstahl's *Triumph of the Will* when Hitler uses the World War I blood flag to sanctify the flags of the SA and SS. But I appreciated, in the pledge, how the sentence moved on from the external sign, the flag, to the essence of the oath, "one nation, under God, indivisible," before it went on to spell out the importance of "liberty and justice for all." Yes, this was something I could pledge my allegiance to—it was different enough from Hitler's formula of *Blut und Boden*, blood and soil.

The oaths and pledges out of the way, we finally sang the national anthem. National anthems weren't my favorite, and I remembered my uncle's witty translation of the German

national anthem into Rotwelsch. But I embraced my new
patriotic duty with diligence. The melody of the U.S. national
anthem is notoriously difficult, perhaps a sign of the musical
aspirations of those who had selected this daring tune with
its leaps and modulations, a vote of confidence in the musical genius of the American people. We newly minted citizens
struggled mightily with the melody, but what we lacked in
musical talent we made up for in enthusiasm because we had
been waiting for this moment for many years. I had received
my green card through the green card lottery, which had been
advertised in Germany under the slogan "American Dream."
After years of being a green card bearer, I was allowed to apply
for citizenship, a process that took about a year and a half and
had finally brought me to the Federal Building on this day.
Others had equally lengthy paths behind them and for many,
those paths had been a great deal rockier than mine. More
than once had I seen immigration officials bully brown and
less-educated immigrants, the browner and the lesser edu-
cated the more harshly, and I knew that almost all of them
had escaped life conditions infinitely harsher than my German
middle-class upbringing.

While we struggled with the melody, at least we had the
lyrics in front of us. The closer I looked, the more puzzled I
became: the lyrics were riddled with mistakes. Some were simple typos. We hailed the star-spangled banner not *at* the twilight's last gleaming but *as* the twilight's last gleaming, which
made no sense since the banner was supposed to rise up in triumph, not disappear with the twilight. Had a frustrated former
English major infiltrated the Department of Homeland Security to sabotage this patriotic song? Other mistakes suggested
the opposite, someone who hadn't mastered the rules of English

grammar at all. Francis Scott Key, the composer of the lyrics, spoke evocatively of the "rockets' red glare," but the Department of Homeland Security simply dropped the apostrophe, thus changing the case from the possessive genitive to the nominative. Other mistakes had to do with punctuation, false or missing commas, semicolons, and question marks. Overall, I counted more than thirty of them.

At first, I felt a kind of outrage: how could the Department of Homeland Security take these important, almost sacred, texts and soil them like this? As "The Star-Spangled [the hyphen, necessary for adjectival phrases, was missing as well] Banner" reminded us, blood had been spilled over these words. Couldn't Homeland Security show a bit more respect? Here we all were, and this was the moment when people from all over the world were being inducted into America through these fundamental texts, but the Department of Homeland Security, which had subjected us to all kinds of tests, including language tests, was failing these tests itself.

Then I looked around and saw that everyone was immersed in singing, and I suddenly felt ashamed. No one cared about the mistakes. Was there anything worse than a know-it-all English professor who just couldn't stop correcting errors at a moment such as this? I snapped out of it and joined the cacophony of America as it was represented on this decrepit floor of the Federal Building. This was how democracy was supposed to sound.

When the anthem was finished, an old television monitor was wheeled into the room and we were shown a prerecorded address from President George W. Bush. Whether by design or not, the sound was turned off, or turned down so much that I couldn't understand a single word. We stared at the small screen and watched Bush's lips move, as in a pantomime. Was this another example of the bureaucracy not caring? Amanda later speculated that New Yorkers were taking their revenge on Bush's misbegotten invasion of Iraq. After the address, we newly minted citizens were finally allowed to reunite with our families, and the celebrations began.

The poor sound quality of President Bush's address was made up for by a letter I received from him, congratulating me on becoming a United States citizen. I was impressed by the White House stationery, with its embossed seal and the simple postal address, consisting of four words, The White House (written in stately dark blue letters) and, on the next line: Washington. That was all. Bush wrote:

> Americans are united across the generations by grand and enduring ideals. The grandest of these ideals is an unfold-ing promise that everyone belongs, that everyone deserves a chance, and that no insignificant person was ever born. Our country has never been united by blood or birth or soil. We are bound by principles that move us beyond our backgrounds, lift us above our interests, and teach us what it means to be citizens. Every citizen must uphold these prin-ciples. And every new citizen, by embracing these ideals, makes our country more, not less, American. . . .
>
> Sincerely,
> George W. Bush

The pedantic professor in me noted that the letter, unlike the materials from the Department of Homeland Security, didn't contain a single mistake, and I was pleased. Even though a few years earlier I had stood for hours in freezing temperatures to protest the impending Second Gulf War, I had always sympathized with President Bush when it came to language. I knew that Bush suffered from dyslexia more severely than I did. He had been attacked, unfairly I felt, for his occasional mistakes. Some of them could be chalked up to the difference between spoken and written language—everyone sounds inarticulate when their spoken words are written down verbatim. Other Bushisms, as they were quickly called, were downright ingenious, for example Bush's famous exclamation: "They misunderestimate me."[1] I think that's exactly what they did. They underestimated Bush because they mistook his struggles with dyslexia for stupidity.

I suspected, of course, that Bush hadn't composed his letter himself, but I found myself taken with his words anyway, especially the observation "Our country has never been united by blood or birth or soil." Getting away from blood, birth, and soil was exactly why I was here, in the United States.

Bush didn't just dismiss blood, birth, or soil. He also assured me that by upholding an ideal of America that went beyond those three retrograde ideas, I was making America even more American than it already was. It was a daring thought. If I understood it correctly—and perhaps I was putting my own, self-serving spin on things—it meant that there was a difference between native-born Americans and naturalized ones. Native-born Americans were Americans because of the accident of their birth. But immigrants like me were here because we had made a choice. We had forsworn allegiance to the soil where we had been born, along with the rulers guarding over it, and had actively opted for the ideals of America, however insufficiently realized. It was okay that the text of the national anthem was full of mistakes, I thought, because it was our job, as immigrants, to correct it.

═══

How exactly had we chosen America? In truth, I don't know exactly why I came here; there were many small reasons, not one big one. My early associations with America are a jumble of scenes and images: a poster of Manhattan in my childhood room; GIs stationed in Nuremberg, hanging out in front of McDonald's (I wasn't allowed to eat there); American movies, invariably dubbed into German, except when they showed in a small theater set up for GIs. Later, in high school, I spent a few summers in the United States, learning English. I got to know Jacksonville, Florida; a small town in eastern Tennessee; the Bay Area; rural Oregon; and Cambridge, Massachusetts. One time, having worked in the hop harvest in Oregon, I took my earnings to New York City and got mugged. The images and experiences were mixed, some disturbing (one family I stayed with included a shell-shocked Vietnam vet). None of it quite added up, but it was very different from what I had grown up with. Perhaps the Puchner instinct of making a rabbit took me here.

I don't know about other rabbits, but this rabbit brought all his baggage from back home. As a German-born American, I felt that Bush's words about blood, birth, and soil were addressed to me more than to others because no country in the history of the world had created a regime more fully and viciously obsessed with blood, birth, and soil than Nazi Germany.

To be sure, after the war, Germany had been rebuilt and was trying slowly, grudgingly, to come to terms with the past by moving beyond a conception of Germany that had no place for vagrants or Jews. In the meanwhile, and somewhat unexpectedly, a different form of migration was taking place.

During the period of rapid economic expansion in the 1950s and 1960s, West Germany recruited immigrant workers, first from Italy and Greece, then from Turkey, to supply the badly needed labor power for what would soon be called the "economic miracle." Ethnic restaurants sprung up here and there, and Germans slowly developed a taste for these foods. On the rare occasions when we went out to a restaurant, we would go to "the Italian" or "the Greek," as we called them. We never went to "the Turk."

My father had many dealings with Turkish immigrants, many of whom worked in the building trades. It was his particular talent to get along with people from all walks of life. When he renovated the house we would move to when I was four years old, he hired Merdan, from Anatolia, to help out. I remember going to the building site and finding the two of them sitting next to each other, each eating a sandwich and sharing a bottle of beer (my mother also invited Merdan to Christmas that year). But my father's strongest bond was with Vural Cokbudak, a fellow architect, to whom he rented the office underneath his own. The two of them would often smoke a pipe and shoot the breeze, and I was delighted when, on rare occasions, I could join them. I don't know what happened to Merdan, but Vural's office remained below my father's until long after my father's death.

In the fall of 1989, I was studying in Konstanz, in the far southwestern corner of Germany. I was sitting in a lecture on linguistics when the professor told us that the Berlin Wall had come down. He was crying. This impressed me more than what I had seen on television. Before long, cheaply made East German cars found their way to Lake Constance, and the following year, a few East German students came to study logic with us—one of them had been trained at the Moscow Institute of Science. It was all very exotic.

I cheered the fact that with the fall of the Soviet Union we had entered a new era of global trade and exchange; those forces had helped Germany change its attitude toward immigrants. In addition, there was now a second generation of German-born Turks (or should they be called Turkish-Germans?), some of whom knew little about Turkey, and it finally dawned on German society in this new global age that these Turks should be given citizenship.

The problem was that they didn't have a drop of "German blood" in their veins. Despite all that had changed in Germany, the definition of citizenship was still primarily based on ethnic origin. It wasn't enough to be born in Germany; you needed to be born of German parentage and able to prove it. After years of political debate, this blood-based definition of citizenship was finally broadened to allow second-generation Turkish-Germans to choose citizenship. Around the same time, they slowly began to make an appearance in public life, from politics to culture and, later still, in soccer (comparable perhaps to the role the integration of baseball played in the United States).

I observed most of these changes from afar, having moved to Italy in the fall of 1992 and then to America in 1993. For me, who tended to see the world through language and literature, the most important turning point came in 1995, when my brother Stephan, a filmmaker and writer who shared many of my interests in language and literature, sent me a small book by the Turkish-German author Feridun Zaimoğlu. The book was called *Kanak Sprak*.[2] *Kanak* was a derogatory term for Turk, and *sprak* was a variant of *Sprache*, the German word for language. *Kanak Sprak*—Zaimoğlu had used the pejorative term for Turkish-German and decided to embrace it. For me, the book was a revelation. It was the first time that I had seen the distinct variant of German that was spoken by Turkish communities appear in literature. I think that my uncle—and Kafka—would have been pleased: Turkish immigrants were "raking up" the German language the way Rotwelsch speakers had done in previous centuries. I gave the book pride of place on my Rotwelsch bookshelf.

===

Meanwhile, some members of my family back home called me "the American," with a slight edge, I felt—especially when I would appear from time to time with yet another piece of startling news: my grandfather's article, his SA membership, his brother's strange career as caretaker of the files from the Nuremberg trials. For them, these were just isolated tidbits from the past. Underneath their lukewarm reactions, I sometimes suspected a skeptical tone, a feeling that I, who had left and had sworn an oath abjuring all adherence to foreign Potentates, including German ones, was now stirring up trouble back in the old country. But perhaps I was just imagining these reactions.

I, in turn, downplayed the personal side of the story whenever I mentioned what I was working on. My official line was: "I'm writing a history of Rotwelsch. I'm using Günter's archive as a source, and perhaps I'll write a bit about him personally."

Initially it was true, of course—that's what I thought I was doing, writing a history of Rotwelsch—but gradually I came to realize that something much more personal was at stake for me. Once, when I had despaired about my Rotwelsch research and was struggling with the book, Amanda had said, with pity in her voice: "Martin, you are writing about your father." It is a thought that sometimes makes me tear up; I don't know what else to do with it.

If immigrating to America shaped my view of what I had left behind, the reverse was also the case. The baggage I brought with me to America—the history of Nazi Germany—shaped how I saw my adopted country. I had embraced the roaring 1990s with its high rates of immigration to America just as I now embraced President Bush's talk of overcoming blood, birth, and soil, but my history also made me take particular note of the realities of post-9/11 America. It was President Bush, after all, who had created the ominously named Department of Homeland Security, a phrase that sounded, to my ears at least, like birth and soil.

More troubling for me was the question of race in America. Nazism had taught me that race didn't exist, and that the only thing that existed was racism, which associated a few superficial features with questions of character, ability, and history. This lesson made me particularly attentive to the history of racism in America, including the demand for reparations. Reparations were a response to harm done in the name of racism, not a claim that racial thinking was justified.

What made less sense to me was a "positive" notion of race. It started with the word "Caucasian." Having researched my grandfather's work of proving our family "Aryan," I was now asked to identify as "Caucasian" on all kinds of forms. I had known this term only as a mountain range in deepest Russia, and now, suddenly, found that it was supposed to be my racial home. The more I looked into it, the more I found that the term "Caucasian" was as heavily tainted by race thinking as "Aryan." The term had been invented by the German "race scientist" Johann Blumenbach, who had visited the Caucasus Mountains and was so taken with the people there that he considered them the highest race, created in God's image. In contrast to Caucasians, Blumenbach dismissed four other races as degenerate: Ethiopians (sub-Saharan Africa); Mongolians (Japan and China); Malays (brown people); and the "red" race (Native Americans). Being labeled a "Caucasian" in this tradition was a strange welcoming to America.

Even more shocking to me was Guantánamo Bay. The history of the Rotwelsch underground was a history of prisons and camps, beginning with Luther's demand that vagabonds be locked up and continuing on to the incarceration of Gregor Gog, the King of the Tramps, in Nazi camps. By going to America, I thought I had left all this safely behind. But now, President Bush, or his administration, had used the ambiguous territorial status of the eastern tip of Cuba, controlled by the United States through a ninety-year lease, to set up a law-free zone in which prisoners could be held indefinitely, out of the reach of the courts, without being charged. This violated the most basic rule of law, and I became obsessed with the place. I followed the Supreme Court cases brought on behalf of various prisoners, some of whom had been picked up more or less randomly on the battlefields of Afghanistan. I attended a working group at Columbia Law School and even wrote a short piece about Guantánamo Bay to grapple with this new reality.[3] (Later I would learn about the deportation camps set up by President Clinton in the mid-1990s.)

Yes, I know: I, too, am suspicious of Nazi comparisons. They are invariably facile and wrong. But what was I supposed to do, having brought my grandfather's ghost with me to America? It wasn't about Nazi comparisons as such; it was about using what I knew, what I had learned during my search, and applying it to the new reality that was taking place around me. This meant that when I looked at Guantánamo Bay, it reminded me—despite all the differences—of Nazi camps because those camps also operated outside the law, taking prisoners who had served their time into indefinite "protective detention," out of fear that they might do harm in the future, without trial. There were many differences between Camp Delta, as it was called, and Nazi concentration camps. The purpose of Camp Delta was not to kill inmates, only to detain, and perhaps to humiliate and to torture them; and the numbers were infinitely smaller. Of the 780 people who have been detained there, only 9 have died, while 731 have been transferred to other prisons or countries, which means that only 40 are left now. In terms of purpose and scale, there was no comparison. The only similarity existed on an extremely abstract level, in the principle of setting up a law-free zone. But I feared, I couldn't help but fear, that once people got used to the principle, it could be expanded, and this thought scared me.

More recently, comparisons of today's America to Nazi Germany appear almost daily in the press, and despite my dislike of such comparisons they have invaded my imagination, and my nightmares. The erosion of democratic institutions feels in some ways similar to what happened during the Weimar Republic in which my grandfather Karl grew up, when conservatives thought they could use Hitler for their own ends, and initially the plan worked beautifully. They were aided by the left, which was hopelessly divided, with Communists convincing themselves that Social Democrats were a worse enemy than Hitler, and vice versa. German conservatives were silent about Hitler's crude politics, thinking that they could have him do their bidding. They were hopelessly wrong, and history has judged them.

What traditional German conservatives, and the divided German left of the early 1930s, didn't realize was that Hitler was wielding new tools, including new communication technologies such as the radio that allowed him to bypass traditional newspapers and speak directly to the people, inaugurating a new form of populism against which the institutions of the state and the press were powerless. His support was especially strong among people who thought the old system was "broken," that Germany was being attacked by migrants from within and rivals from without, that it was being bullied on the world stage, exploited even by its alleged allies, and that what Germany needed above all was respect.

When I use what I know about Rotwelsch to look at our world today, I can't help but notice that a similar tone, similar phrases, similar ideas have returned. The old enemies of Rotwelsch are resurgent, especially in Germany, Austria, and Eastern Europe, where the lessons of the Nazi era have waned and right-wing nationalism, xenophobia, and attacks on Sinti and Roma and on migration in all of its forms are on the rise. The rebirth of anti-immigration nationalism isn't confined to Central and Eastern Europe. It has occurred all over the world, manifesting itself in attacks on migrants and minorities, from Christians in Egypt to Poles in England, Syrians in Poland, and Roma everywhere. Rotwelsch embodies the principle of migration in its purest form. Undocumented was the original condition of Rotwelsch speakers, why they had to forge their papers, as Baumhauer did, to navigate a world hostile to vagrancy.

There can be no doubt that migration, documented and undocumented, will increase in the future. Even the most optimistic predictions of the consequences of climate change or other major disruptions include massive migration. As new and greater populations are forced into the underground, we are fostering the growth of new migratory languages, and these new languages are in turn fostering what Gog, the King of the Tramps, called self-awareness, the knowledge that the undocumented belong to a new and growing class of migrants that stretches to many parts of the world.

What if Rotwelsch wasn't a historical curiosity, but a harbinger of the future?

ROTWELSCH LESSON:
THE AMERICAN OATH OF ALLEGIANCE

I dibber, and gable, that I will rat on any welsch baldower, schiankel, martine zi kohl which I have geschomst.

I hereby declare, under oath, that I absolutely, and entirely, renounce and abjure all allegiance and fidelity to any Foreign Prince, Potentate, State or Sovereignty of whom or of which I have heretofore been a subject or citizen.

(Literal translation: I say, and swear, that I will betray [there is no word in Rotwelsch for allegiance or fidelity] all foreign leaders, kings, and states which I used to serve.)

Dibbern = to talk, to say
Gabeln = to swear
Rat = to betray (Romani)

Welsch = foreign; incomprehensible

Baldower = scout or leader

Schiankel = master (Romani): disgusting

Schomsen = to serve (past participle of this verb is
   geschomst)

Chapter 13

YOUR GRANDFATHER WOULD HAVE BEEN PROUD OF YOU

———

There was one person I had not yet interviewed about my family's strange relationship to Rotwelsch: Roswitha. I had postponed the moment when I would talk to her, perhaps because of the hesitant reactions of other family members to my questions, or because I worried that what I had discovered would be painful to her. But I knew that she would be a great source on the Puchner family's past. Though over a decade younger, Roswitha had been around, or at least nearby, during the most dramatic moments in her brothers' lives. Should I call her? Or write her a letter? Somehow, it never seemed like the best moment.

Fortunately, in the fall of 2017 Roswitha decided to visit me. I was worried that she wouldn't make it up to my fourth-floor walkup in Brooklyn. With her niece Franziska's help, she climbed the narrow stairs, one flight at a time, with barely any pauses in between, despite her recent hip replacement surgery. I had always admired her perseverance. At a relatively young age, she had lost her father, her brother, her mother, and eventually her other brother (my father). At the same time, she had gotten married, started a university career in music, raised a son, gotten a divorce, changed careers, and opened a bookstore.

During my father's funeral, I had looked at her and thought, She is the last Puchner of her generation. But it was only a momentary recognition before I fell again into the tangle of my own grief. I thought of this moment when she appeared at my door, panting heavily—she was my most direct connection to the past.

Franziska and Roswitha were interested in the fact that I was writing about Rotwelsch, but they didn't understand exactly why I was doing it, although they were too polite to say so. I didn't blame them because I didn't quite know myself. Perhaps they were used to it—this was what happened in the Puchner family; someone might get infected with the Rotwelsch bug and suffer for the rest of his life. The best strategy was to show polite interest, but not too much; in the worst-case scenario, you might get roped into writing dictionaries at night, as had happened to Franziska's mother, my aunt Heidi.

For over twenty years, I had wondered whether Günter knew about his father's anti-Rotwelsch article and how Karl reacted as he watched his son devote his life to this language. Cautiously, I asked whether Roswitha remembered any tension between her brother and his father around Rotwelsch. "No," she said. The thought had clearly never crossed her mind. "On the contrary: he inherited the interest in obscure historical names from his father."

Years ago, when I had posed the same question to Heidi, Günter's widow, she had reacted similarly. How could that be? Had they been completely oblivious to the Rotwelsch war within their family? Or had Karl been able to keep his opinions about Rotwelsch and Yiddish to himself? Did he think, as Roswitha clearly did, that Günter was essentially following his father's occupation? Did Karl say, "I am so proud of you, son: you are continuing my legacy with your studies of Rotwelsch names"?

Before I could ask what she knew about her father's Nazi past, she started to reminisce about him, the professor of history and researcher in obscure names. She mentioned some of his charming eccentricities, the foibles of someone peddling obscure knowledge. She also told us how thrilled he had been when, early on in her university career, she started teaching at the same university where he had studied and where he taught after his rehabilitation. "It was his last semester of teaching, and I had just begun teaching. He picked up the course catalogue, and both of our names were in it. He was very pleased, and proud."

More than a decade younger than her two brothers, Roswitha had been less involved in their rebellions and reckonings. She saw herself as the one who had followed in her father's footsteps by getting a Ph.D., the only one of the three siblings to do so, and pursuing a university career. Her father had worked himself up from his own petit bourgeois upbringing, the first in his family to go to college. It made sense that he must have hoped his sons would follow a similar path. But they had chosen their bohemian lifestyles. Then, the youngest comes along, and finally there is a child who continues the academic tradition of the family by studying medieval music. It had to be medieval, I thought, something little known, not one of the obvious blockbusters like Mozart or Beethoven or, God forbid, contemporary music. Two seminars, his on medieval manuscripts, hers on medieval musical manuscripts, at the prestigious Ludwig

Maximilian University. "He was so proud," Roswitha repeated once more.

I was still thinking this through, figuring out when I should tell my aunt about the photograph and the anti-Semitic article, when I said weakly, "But what about Rotwelsch?" She misunderstood, thinking that I was asking her about my own project: "Your grandfather would have been so proud of you. You are the one in your generation who is following in his footsteps."

"Me?" I exclaimed. "He would be proud of me?" I got up abruptly to clear the table and busy myself with the dishes. I was too surprised and confused to say anything more. How could this possibly be the case? I realized that ever since that moment in Widener Library more than twenty years earlier when I had begun my search into Rotwelsch and the family's past, I had cast my Nazi grandfather as a villain. He had tried to keep German, and Germany, pure. He had hidden his past, the past that I had finally dragged out into the open. And now, my aunt was suggesting that I, the one who fearlessly pursued the truth, who wasn't taken in by family stories, who dug up documents and evidence, hunted for lies and omissions, who exposed the whitewashing of the past, I, who had secretly thought of myself as the hero of our story, was like him?

Roswitha's point about my uncle, how he was in some ways similar to his father, was easier to comprehend. I had already begun to suspect it, the more I thought about archives and the personalities and motivations of people who kept them. While Günter must have disappointed his father by not becoming an academic and instead continuing with his bohemian life as a musician and poet, he had spent considerable time constructing a Rotwelsch library and archive. A clear line of influence led from one archivist to another, from a father who had devoted his life to researching old names and meanings to a son who had done the same.

Suddenly, a new series of scenarios flashed through my mind, of Günter getting technical advice from his father about his archive and how to organize it, of evenings in which they both pored over names and their derivations, tracking etymologies and histories. Perhaps Karl was as pleased with his oldest son's interest in historical documents and names as he was with his daughter's academic path. It was almost as if he started a dynasty of archivists and professors, which my father would belatedly join, when he began to teach at the technical university in Nuremberg. Before his death, Karl could look back and see that despite his Nazi past, despite his having abandoned his family, despite the rebellion of his sons, his children had chosen professions that continued what he had begun.

I had trouble making conversation with my aunt and cousin for the rest of the evening and was glad when they went back to their hotel, leaving me to mull over what I had heard. It was unexpected but, when seen from a distance, undeniable. I was precisely the kind of academic my grandfather would have appreciated; in my generation, I am the only one who routinely spends time in archives, to study old documents, to delve into obscure corners of the past. That is why it was I, and not another member of my family, who had ended up reading Karl's file, even though my brother Stephan and my cousins lived within walking distance of his archive. It took someone who was like Karl to become the world's only expert on Rotwelsch.

Throughout my conversation with my aunt, my cousin Franziska had been listening. She didn't talk much about her father, Günter, who had died when she was in her early teens, nor did I know whether his professional and personal life choices had influenced her, but it now occurred to me that she had chosen to work as a professional translator. Did she see a connection between her father's translation project and her own professional path?

Early on in college, I had taken a course on deciphering medieval manuscripts. I can't for the life of me reconstruct what I was doing there. There was no reason for me to study medieval manuscripts, and to my fellow students it sounded almost like a willful attempt to study something maximally useless. But there I was, learning different types of writing, slowly trying to make sense of a scribe's hand as if planning on a career as an archivist.

One day, after class, the professor took me aside to ask whether I was related to Karl Puchner. I said that I was. He seemed pleased. "You are continuing the family tradition," he said, chuckling to himself. "Well, not really," I laughed. "I'm in the philosophy department. I'm taking this course just for fun." "Fun?" he said. Even to him, who presumably enjoyed his profession, this didn't seem like a sufficient explanation. I didn't ponder this exchange at the time and had forgotten about it until my aunt's remark.

As I was lying awake that night, I worked myself around to recognizing that my aunt was right: my grandfather would have been proud of me. True, he had lashed out against Rotwelsch, making common cause with the Nazis. But I had no idea what that meant to him afterward, what differences we might have had. Did he hold on to his earlier Nazi beliefs, or did he, retrospectively, see his involvement with the Nazis as an aberration, as he claimed in his de-Nazification files, a misguided attempt to make his obscure scholarly interests "relevant" to the political climate of the time?

Or perhaps he hoped simply to bring his arcane subject matter to a general public. Probably he had previously received
nothing but laughs and good-humored condescension whenever the topic of his studies came up. Karl with his old names
and meanings, his manuscripts and documents. How could
someone devote his life to something so irrelevant? Then,
suddenly, as the political ground shifted and the question of
names became a hot topic, he saw his chance to bring his hard-
earned knowledge—along with the ugly emotions that led him
to hate or fear Jews, migrants, people insufficiently German—
to the political questions of his time. I recognized myself in
this desire to take obscure research and make it relevant. It's
almost inevitably the lot of academics to hope, against all rea-
sonable expectations, that whatever topic of research we've
been obsessing about might be seen as not purely "academic"—
the word itself signals irrelevance. I find it crucial to expose
my ideas to broader scrutiny. I encourage my students to do
the same, I even teach other academics how to reach a broader
audience. "If we believe that what we do is important," I thun-
der, "we must make every effort to bring our work to a larger
public." Isn't this conviction one of the reasons I am writing
this book, hoping that a reckoning with Nazi Germany and
thinking about migration in Central Europe might have lessons for us here in America today? No matter how convinced
I was of the difference between us, this thought left me with a
bitter aftertaste, a feeling that here was yet another similarity
between me and my grandfather that I didn't know what to do
with.

═══

The next day, Roswitha and Franziska came to visit me at the New York Public Library, where I was doing research on Rotwelsch. I showed them my small office; they cast passing glances at my books, then I took them upstairs to the stunning Rose Reading Room, one of the largest interior rooms without columns in the world. While they were admiring the richly ornamented ceiling, I directed their attention to my favorite feature of the NYPL: the train that runs through the entire building and brings the books from the stacks downstairs to the counters where they are delivered to the people who requested them. It's a little bigger than a toy train: the carts are about two feet long and six inches wide and are suspended from a single arm. This means that when they run up and down a steep incline, the contraption holding the books rights itself automatically so that the books don't fall out. The stacks are built deep into the ground and extend beyond the building underneath Bryant Park. While office workers and tourists mingle on the lawn above, deep down underneath them librarians select books and put them on the toy trains that take them up through the empty stacks into the reading room.

When Roswitha, Franziska, and I returned to my office, I showed them what the train had brought up for me a few weeks earlier: the complete run of the journal my father and my uncle had published from their communal apartment in the sixties. I had seen individual issues of the journal before, but I'd never seen them all bound together and I'd never seen them outside a Puchner family home. The print run can't have been more than a few hundred, perhaps less than that; mostly the journal was distributed among friends and at a few bookstores and pubs. How had this extremely obscure literary journal made it across the Atlantic and into the bowels of the New York Public Library? My aunt and cousin seemed pleased, but somehow their reaction wasn't quite as awed as I had hoped it would be.

I had planned to continue the conversation from the night before and finally tell Roswitha what I'd learned about her father, but I found myself hesitating again. Instead, I chatted with her and my cousin for a bit, and then I took them down the grand staircase and out to the wild honking of Fifth Avenue.

When I returned to my study, I was ashamed that my campaign against silence had now, finally, encountered a silence it was not willing to break: my own.

ROTWELSCH LESSON:
HOW TO AVOID A SUBJECT IN ROTWELSCH

Cartouchen = to deceive (from the name of Louis Dominique Cartouche, a master *gonef*)

Ebbes dibbern = to speak vaguely (Yiddish *dabr*, to speak)

Färben = to lie (literally, to dye something)

Flachsen = to flatter, to lie

Flöten = to speak in a friendly way (literally, to play the flute); *flöte* (flute) = a stupid person

Kauderwelsch dibbern = to speak nonsense

Kaspern = to talk, to deceive

Kohlen = to tell a story, to lie (literally, to coal; from Romani, *kalo*, black)

Kosak = a cheat (after Cossack, a people of Ukraine)

Lamden = clever thief (Yiddish, *lamdn*, scholar)

Mamser = a traitor (Yiddish, *mamzer*, bastard)

Mauscheln = to deceive (originally a derogatory term for speaking Yiddish)

Menkenke = to talk around an issue

Schmäh = a tale, a lie (possibly from Yiddish *shmie*, sense of hearing)

Chapter 14

ROTWELSCH IN AMERICA

———

In 2007, the year I became a U.S. citizen, I, along with many of my fellow Americans, enjoyed the first season of *Mad Men*. Toward the end of the season, there is a flashback to Don Draper's childhood. He is living on a farm with his mean stepfather when a hobo comes by and works for a day in exchange for room, board, and a quarter. The stepfather cheats the hobo out of the quarter and the hobo leaves in anger. Young Don Draper accompanies him to the road and watches him carve a sign into a tree. The hobo explains to the boy that the sign means that a bad man lives here.

When I saw the sign, I almost leaped from my chair. "I know this sign," I shouted. Amanda, who doesn't like watching TV but reads about the shows afterward, ran into the living room to see what had happened. "I know the sign," I repeated, pointing at the TV. "What are you saying?" Amanda said, and I realized that the film had moved on. "They used a Rotwelsch *zinken* on *Mad Men*," I explained. "It's the same sign I grew up with."

Amanda looked skeptical and left. She probably thought that my obsession with Rotwelsch was becoming worrisome.

Zinken had made it to America, presumably in the nineteenth century, a time of renewed immigration from German-speaking lands, when Rotwelsch speakers came here (as Konstanzer Hans had wanted to do), bringing their language and their *zinken* with them. But the high tide of hobo *zinken* came during the Great Depression, when they were used in much the same way that Central European itinerants had used them: to navigate the difficult life on the road. The signs were adapted to suit the needs of their new users. American hoboes sometimes walked the road, but they also sneaked rides on trains, and some signs helped them navigate that mode of transportation.

My uncle had been onto this story of migration as well. Among his books, I found a slim volume from 1974 listing the most common American hobo signs. It included many I knew from childhood, such as the WW for an aggressive dog, the bars warning of jail time, the cross recommending that you act piously, and the X with a circle around it that had directed vagrants to my childhood home. Rotwelsch signs had followed me to America, or rather, they had preceded me, greeting me upon my arrival like an old friend.

In the post–World War II world, American *zinken* slowly declined. The book of hobo signs in my uncle's library was subtitled: "A lament for the demise of the most communicative symbolism of them all." It continued: "Drawn largely from the symbolism of medieval magic and the mystic alphabet of the Cabala, these signs have been in widespread use even in America until recent times of general affluence."[1] This scholar was reaching all the way back to the Kabbalistic tradition, which I had encountered in the attic of the Old-New Synagogue of Prague. Clearly, the connection between *zinken* and religious symbols had captured his imagination as much as it had captured mine.

Once I started to look for traces of Rotwelsch and *zinken*, I found them hidden all over the place. It turns out that the Jewish gangs of New York called a whorehouse *nafke bias* (*nafke*, Aramaic for difference; *nekeyve*, woman; *bayes* means house), a thief *gonef*, and prison *shul* (*schul*, in Rotwelsch), just as Central European Rotwelsch speakers had done. They were also accustomed to my old favorite, "being in a pickle." It is difficult to say whether these terms and expressions had filtered into English from Rotwelsch or from Yiddish. Most Yiddish speakers who had immigrated to America had come from Eastern Europe, beyond the Rotwelsch sphere of influence, which ended somewhere in the outer reaches of the Hapsburg Empire, east of Vienna and Prague. That did not stop me from telling my American friends that they, too, had been speaking Rotwelsch all along, getting into pickles, and watching television in which hobo *zinken* played a central role. (The influence in the nineteenth and early twentieth centuries went both ways: there was a Rotwelsch word for Coca-Cola, *koksplemp*.)

In search for more Rotwelsch traces in my new homeland, I contacted the Endangered Language Alliance (ELA) in New York. If ever there was an endangered language, it was Rotwelsch, hunted by the police from the beginning of its existence and all the way to the Third Reich. Yet it didn't even appear on the UNESCO list of endangered languages. Most likely, Rotwelsch was not only endangered but already dead.

The ELA is located in an office building in Midtown Manhattan. I reached it by means of a cargo elevator that deposited me in two rooms overflowing with old computers, filing cabinets, and interns. The co-director, a linguist by the name of Ross Perlin, explained to me that the purpose of the organization was to preserve—and possibly to revitalize—dying languages. Of the seven thousand existing languages, half are expected to vanish before the end of the century. Ross directed me to their website, which explains that preserving knowledge of these dying languages is a crucial mission because "every language carries with it immense reserves of cultural, historical, ecological, and botanical information, vital for local communities and potentially to the broader world."[2]

The caveat "potentially to the broader world" was there because of a long-standing controversy among linguists. In the early twentieth century, as part of the linguistic turn, anthropologically oriented linguists had claimed that each language carries with it a distinct way of seeing the world. The way a language uses tenses shapes our sense of time; the way it uses spatial relations shapes our sense of geography; its words for

emotions, values, and social relations shape all of those per-
ceptions. There is nothing in our view of the world that isn't
influenced by the specific language we speak. This theory was
perfect for projects like the Endangered Language Alliance
because it meant that with every language that disappeared, so,
too, did a distinct view of the world.

The theory, sometimes called linguistic relativism, has
come under attack. Psychologists found that there are important areas of perception and cognition that work independently
from specific languages, even independently from language as
such. (Some of these corrections were based on experiments
with people who lost their ability to speak or process language.)
Other claims about language-determined ideas of time and
space were difficult to prove and came to be seen as overreach,
a typical case of professional deformation: linguists believing
that language shapes everything. (I am highly susceptible to
this syndrome as well.)

Faced with this debate, organizations such as the ELA have
learned to tread more carefully, emphasizing the importance of
preserving languages for their speakers and for our knowledge
of the human past but only "potentially" for larger questions
such as how we see the world. I think they were right to avoid
overblown arguments because they don't need them. Even if
each language doesn't carry with it a distinct way of seeing the
world, each language is still a human-made artifact of astonishing complexity that should be preserved. As the linguist Ken
Hale, an inspiration for ELA, put it: letting hundreds or even
thousands of languages disappear was like "dropping a bomb on
the Louvre."[3]

The place where that bomb was being defused, at ELA, was
a small, soundproof cubicle in which remaining speakers of

endangered languages could be recorded. Perlin explained that New York was the best place for embarking on this project. He estimated that of the seven thousand endangered languages, as many as eight hundred had speakers living in the New York area. To drive home this point, ELA had recently landed a publicity coup with a map called "Mother Tongues and Queens." Based on six years of work, it captured the linguistic riches of New York by focusing on the city's borough with the largest number of immigrants.

Perlin called New York a "last-minute Babel." New York had entered this era of hyperdiversity after 1965, when immigration laws that had discriminated against most emigrants from the developing world were finally revised. As a consequence, immigration to the United States increased and, more important, the number of countries from which immigrants came to America increased as well. It was fortuitous timing. Just at the moment when the pace of the great language extinction was picking up, immigrants from the largest possible range of language backgrounds were drawn to this one city. All Perlin had to do was find them and lure them to his recording booth. It was a case of historical luck, but time was running out and this one chance needed to be seized.

When I first got in touch with ELA, I had secretly hoped that I might join this group and get my own little pin on the map. Couldn't Perlin record me in his booth speaking some Rotwelsch phrases? Wasn't I, very likely, the last speaker of Rotwelsch in the world? I found the romance, the tragic heroism of this position, the idea that I was the last line of defense between the bomb and the Louvre, immensely appealing.

When I actually sat across from him in his office, with all the interns milling about, I didn't dare utter this thought because I

realized how silly it was. I wasn't a real Rotwelsch speaker. I had
no business being on a map of "Mother Tongues and Queens"
for the simple reason that I had not grown up speaking Rotwelsch as my mother tongue (also, I wasn't living in Queens).
At best I could claim to have grown up "around" Rotwelsch,
with a few dozen Rotwelsch terms and phrases and as many
Rotwelsch *zinken*, having used them here and there as a party
trick. So what if Rotwelsch shaped my life, from my early fascination with languages to my studies in linguistics and literature
and all the way to my research into the careers of my uncle and
my grandfather? This only meant that Rotwelsch was important to me personally, and not to a "community," as the ELA
demanded, or "the broader world."

Instead of trying to get into the booth, I told Perlin a bit
about Rotwelsch and why it fascinated me. Immediately his
eyes lit up and he recalled other underground languages, some
extinct, some still spoken in places from China and Iran to
London. I had always thought of Rotwelsch as a unique language mixture created for a particular form of life on the road.
It turned out that while Rotwelsch was unique in its specifics,
there existed many languages like it.

One was Zargari, the language of Iranian Roma that became
the language of goldsmiths and artisans and was seen as secret
because this sociolect was incomprehensible to the general population. There was also Lomavren, a mixture of Romani and
Armenian spoken by certain groups of Roma in the Caucasus. I
came upon a language of horse traders that partially overlapped
with Rotwelsch. But closest to Rotwelsch, and singled out by
Perlin, was Lotera'i, a language spoken by Jewish communities
in Persia.[4] Like Rotwelsch, it was a language that used a large
number of Hebrew words not understood by surrounding gen-

tiles, who were Farsi speakers. The only significant difference was that this language remained tied to a particular community, not like Rotwelsch, which had become a lingua franca spoken by whoever had drifted into the underground.

In talking to Perlin, I realized that I didn't have to venture all the way to Persia in search of Rotwelsch-like languages. If all marginalized groups developed their own way of talking, often incomprehensible to outsiders, then versions of Rotwelsch and its *zinken* must exist everywhere (or rather, Rotwelsch was an example of something much larger). Some Rotwelsch scholars, whether driven by hostile intents or not, had noticed the same thing. My main source for Czech Rotwelsch, Karl Treimer, writing in 1937, listed as kindred examples the languages of the stock exchange, the racetrack, professional sports, the film business, ragpickers, horse traders, pickpockets, the Foreign Legion, hunters, sailors, paprika sellers, students, chauffeurs, pathfinder, prison inmates, typesetters, soldiers, vintners, and Jews.[5]

Inspired by this list, I looked around me and recognized the impulse behind *zinken* in the tattoos of gangs, and the impulse behind Rotwelsch in the special language of skateboarders, the lingo of teenagers, the vocab of rappers, and the obscure terms of hackers. Should I even include the (regular) Latin of doctors, the jargon of professors, the obfuscations of lawyers? Encouraged by Treimer's reference to the stock exchange, I came across the language that emerged from court documents related to the bankruptcy of Lehman Brothers. Traders had developed a deliberately obscure language to downplay risk, a white-collar Rotwelsch of Wall Street.[6]

A source for some of today's sociolects is the Urban Dictionary, a website started in 1999 as an attempt to collect different jargons spoken by college students in California. Open to anyone who wanted to contribute, the website exploded in size and range; decisions about inclusion were crowd-sourced. Even though the founder, Aaron Peckham, who is still the site's only employee, sought to keep out obvious pranks, the difference between a legitimate piece of jargon and a spoof was never quite clear, and the entire site lived, quite happily, in a gray zone of illegitimacy. The point of the Urban Dictionary wasn't to gain legitimacy for these expressions. It was to document the inventiveness of niche languages, the creative energy behind language innovation from below.

While the Endangered Language Alliance spoke of languages as cultural artworks, on a par with paintings in the Louvre, other organizations spoke of linguistic diversity as a form of biodiversity, comparing the extinction of languages with the extinction of species. There was something immensely appealing in that comparison, which made languages seem like rare butterflies that must be protected from predators. Languages were no longer created by humans, like paintings in the Louvre, but by nature, which also made them part of an ecosystem. Destroying a language meant not only destroying a species but also threatening the entire ecosystem, which might be overrun by an invasive species, like English or another dominant language, destroying its carefully calibrated balance. Weren't imported languages like that, foreign and invasive, wiping out any number of local languages?

I have come to distrust these analogies. Rotwelsch has taught me that languages are tools for survival that allowed, for example, members of the itinerant underground to navigate life on the road, tools that gave humans a decisive advantage because they enabled them to cooperate much more effectively, both within groups and across generations, preserving knowledge and passing it on, first through oral traditions and then, in the last five thousand years, through writing.

Contemplating this extraordinary tool returned me to the debate about linguistic relativism. I realized that the terms of the debate had been lopsided. It wasn't so much that the structure of a particular language imposed its own distinct way of perceiving the world. It was the reverse: a specific lived environment had found expression in the language spoken by its members. They had developed a particular idiom for their own purposes, which meant that their purposes, their form of life, could be reconstructed from that language. This was what I had done with Rotwelsch, using it as a guide to the lives of its users. Their words for police, for being arrested, their *zinken* about begging and stealing, the rich vocabulary of food, drink, sex and lice, all this spoke volumes about their lived experience. Rotwelsch was like a worn tool that bore the traces of its earlier use. By studying it closely, one could tell a lot about the bodies that had wielded it.

The theory that languages are tools used for particular purposes, sometimes for many different purposes, means that extinct languages belong neither in a museum of art nor in a museum of natural history. Tools are meant to be surpassed by better tools. Once they are, they should be preserved in a museum of technology, of human ingenuity, of the cultural past.

====

The idea that languages are tools comes from my favorite language philosopher: Ludwig Wittgenstein. Of all theorists of language, I associate him most closely with my father, perhaps because I first encountered Wittgenstein in 1989, when my parents took me to Vienna. There was much my father wanted to show me, especially the architecture there. We crisscrossed the city looking for buildings that were on the cusp between the rich ornamentation of the nineteenth century and the austere geometries of modernism.

My father's favorite building in Vienna was a house Wittgenstein built for his sister. It was designed in an uncompromisingly modernist style that consisted of several cubes pushed together, with strictly geometric windows that had no frames, balconies, or any other type of ornament. On the outside, the house contained only what was necessary: rectangular walls with holes for windows and for one door. There were no colors either; it was painted white.

The interior was austere, but more elegant. The floor-to-ceiling windows looked much larger than they had from the outside, flooding the house with light. There were no curtains or shutters. In their stead I discovered an impressive hydraulic construction sunk into the floor, with steel panels that could be pulled out to cover up windows. All of these details were designed by Wittgenstein himself. My father especially loved the doorknobs and the window latches: they were simple, reduced to their basic function.

Wittgenstein's evolving view of language was similar. Language, he came to realize, is embedded in a particular form of life, a particular experience of being in the world. This meant that one needed to study the functions and purposes it had for its actual users.[7]

Strangely, Wittgenstein had gone to the same school as Adolf Hitler; the two would even have been classmates. There is no record of their interacting, and they would have run in

different circles, with Wittgenstein coming from extreme priv-
ilege and Hitler being the son of a lowly government employee.[8]
After this shared schooling, Hitler would drift into the halfway
houses of Vienna, possibly encountering Rotwelsch and, later,
would rant against Yiddish and Esperanto. Wittgenstein would
go on to celebrate the varieties of languages and the lives lived
by their speakers.

Wittgenstein has been in the back of my mind ever since I
started working on this book because Rotwelsch must be the
single best argument for a tool-based understanding of language. When I look back at the Wittgenstein house, I see the
connection between its rigorous modernism and Wittgenstein's
later philosophy of language even more clearly. Wittgenstein
knew his sister and her needs, including the need to secure her
windows. The house was custom-tailored for a particular person, and it was designed with that use in mind, for the kind of
life that would be lived in it. Over time, Wittgenstein came to
see language in the same way.

=====

All my life I had thrown myself into learning new languages
and learning about languages, but I hadn't spent much time
thinking about the loss of a language. How did it feel, the slow
slipping away of words, as a language disappears? It's an experience everyone who has learned languages as an adult, and who
has made it into middle age, will know. We forget languages,
especially those we don't use.

Ross Perlin at the ELA had said something else about endangered languages: that we live in a golden age of language revival.
The reason is technology. To revive a language, you need a dic-

tionary (lexicon), a grammar (syntax), and a recording (phonetics). It has never been easier to record, you don't even need to go to Perlin's studio. Just take out your phone, visit your grandmother, and you're set. With a dictionary, a grammar, and a recording, a language can be brought to life again, if only there's enough will to see the project through. Hebrew had become largely a language of scripture, although it lived on in Yiddish and Rotwelsch. But then, it was revived in the nineteenth century as the language that should be spoken in Palestine. Welsh is barely spoken in traditional farming communities anymore, but it's now studied with zeal in schools because it has become a requirement for obtaining certain government posts. Other languages have been on the verge of extinction but are kept alive through the commitment of language groups, schools, and states.

But no state will come to the rescue of Rotwelsch, which has always been at odds with all states as well as with national and ethnic identities. I can tell myself a million times that there are other special languages like it, other sociolects, other underground jargons, but I still can't get over the fact that this particular language will likely disappear.

What will endure, I hope, is the idea of Rotwelsch, the idea that marginalized groups develop special languages as tools for survival. We often think of such groups in terms of ethnic identity, but the identity of Rotwelsch speakers was defined by being outside the order of settled society, period. From this position as complete outsiders, they forged an identity by borrowing from the languages around them, with astonishing resilience and inventiveness. Having been cast out from society, they created an idiom that expressed their hard-earned wisdom, their willingness to live differently, and their sheer will to survive.

Capturing the resilience and humanity of its speakers, Rotwelsch is a monument to the endurance of generations of ultimate outcasts. Even if Rotwelsch itself is disappearing, there are
new versions of it springing up everywhere, nomadic languages
spoken by people on the move. One might look for these new
languages in the margins of state power, in areas where settled
society is weak or in retreat. One might find them in places
where people from different origins are thrown together in
communities that must struggle for survival, in places to which
we normally avert our eyes, such as the refugee camps along
contested borders.

But these new Rotwelsch languages are spoken not only in
faraway places that most of us can safely ignore. They are spoken nearby, on migration routes cutting through open country,
in safe houses, and the underground of large cities. New types
of Rotwelsch are spoken, also, in encrypted chatrooms used by
global migrants who adapt dominant languages in their own
ways, developing new common idioms of the underground.
Rotwelsch, the idea of Rotwelsch, is everywhere.

If I have learned anything from studying Rotwelsch, it is that
we, the settlers, the people with passports and states, the ones
who own territories, should not seek to control this language;
perhaps we shouldn't even record it, since the history of studying Rotwelsch is so closely associated with attempts to suppress
it. Above all, we should not view it as a threat to our existing
order. It was fear, I have come to believe, that created the history of persecution and hatred of outsiders, who are so easily
seen as a threat. Perhaps the best we can do is modify this fear
into an acceptance of difference, and to view Rotwelsch as a
reminder that our settled lives are not the only way of organizing existence, that there are people who are unsettled, whether

from necessity or choice. Every order, if it is to avoid becoming oppressive, must accept disorder, every border must accept porousness, every state must accept statelessness. Learning to live with Rotwelsch—this is a task worth pursuing. It's the task I have chosen for myself.

ROTWELSCH LESSON:

ROTWELSCH FOR AMERICA

Amerikanische Martine = USA
Amerikanisch mischen = a scam in which a player pretends
    to be shuffling cards
Koksplemp = Coca-Cola
Chuzpe = impudence; daring
Goi = non-Jew
Gonef = thief
In a pickle = in dire straits
Luft (air) = liberty
Malochn = to work (Yiddish, *melokhe*, work, handicraft)
Massematten = trade, legal and illegal
Massel = luck
Moos = money

Chapter 15

THE LAUGHTER OF
A YENISH CHIEF

In the summer of 2019, a newspaper published an article about my Rotwelsch project, prompting people write to me to with tidbits of information about this language. One writer remembered that he had inherited a Rotwelsch dictionary but had since lost track of it. Did I know about this work? Another sent me an article on a gesture I hadn't known, a hand making a quick circle, which meant to steal something. Called "making a bohemian circle," the gesture had originated in the Vienna underworld and was most likely used by Rotwelsch speakers and their descendants.[1]

Encouraged by this lead, I came across an Austrian sociologist by the name of Roland Girtler, who had done research in the Vienna underworld among vagrants, prostitutes, and pimps. Rejecting the dominant mode of doing quantitative research using questionnaires, Girtler instead hung out with members of the underground and slowly won their trust. In the course of his research, Girtler noticed that people in this milieu were speaking, as late as the 1980s and '90s, a sociolect that contained Rotwelsch words. He started to study the history of the language, drawing on some of the sources I had used as well.[2]

There were further sightings of Rotwelsch. The mayor of Schillingsfürst, a small town in Bavaria, wrote to say that the town was proud of its association with Rotwelsch and that it contained speakers of a later variant of the language, called Yenish. It was the term used by my uncle in his last, unpublished work to designate the descendants of Rotwelsch speakers in this particular region. Another writer reported that he had conducted an archaeological dig in Bopfingen, a small town in southern Germany, some twenty years ago. Looking for local help with the digging, he had come across a group of people who were camped out on the mountainside below the castle. When these workers were among themselves, they spoke an incomprehensible language he suspected was Rotwelsch.

Clearly, remnants of Rotwelsch had taken up residence in different parts of Austria and southern Germany. The language was in peril, but it wasn't dead.

The most extensive email exchange took place with François Miche, a member of the General Council of Fribourg, in the French-speaking part of Switzerland. His grandfather had given shelter to vagrants during World War II, and Miche had inherited a deep sympathy for their descendants, who had never forgotten the help they had received from the family. He met with them regularly, functioned as an unofficial advisor to one of their leaders, and had even written about them, not always to the delight of the authorities.

Yenish- and, to some extent, Rotwelsch-speaking vagrants, it turned out, had survived in Switzerland because the country had remained neutral during the war and had thus been spared the Nazi prosecution of Rotwelsch speakers taking place in other parts of Europe. This didn't mean that Swiss vagrants were treated well. After the war, there had been a process of enforced settlement, a typical example of the state imposing a mixed bag of welfare provisions and force onto nomadic peoples, threatening their lifestyle and culture.

There was one aspect of this culture that received official recognition, however: its language. Switzerland had always been a multilanguage state, with four official languages: German; French; Italian; and Romansh, a Romance language spoken by about 50,000 inhabitants living high up in the mountains close to Italy. In addition to these four languages, Switzerland recognized Yenish as a language without territory.

Despite the efforts to force nomads to adopt a sedentary life, there still existed, Miche wrote, small groups of nomadic peoples in Switzerland today. In fact, there was increasing interest among some to return to the nomadic lifestyle of old, a reaction against the enforced settlement programs of previous decades.

These remaining, or perhaps even growing, groups of nomads were rarely recognized as such, he went on, because they sought to evade any form of official recognition. Sometimes, this was due to the ignorance of the state, which tended to group them with Sinti or Roma and regarded their language as a strange variant of Romani, repeating a common misunderstanding that was several hundred years old. Sometimes, members of nomadic groups even encouraged this confusion when encountering officials and scholars whose motives for studying their language they distrusted; there were cases when nomads had mischievously recited words from Romani dictionaries to eager researchers to obscure their actual language. Once, when Miche had written something about the language, members of the group had asked him to remove it, hoping to keep their language secret. Such evasive tactics were born from hard experience. All too often, scholars and the police had worked hand in hand, as I had found as well, so that hiding from the one also included misleading the other. This deep instinct for secrecy also meant that once a Yenish or Rotwelsch word had filtered into the majority language, it tended to fall out of use among its original speakers.

Hearing these descriptions made me realize that secrecy was far more important than I had come to believe. Miche's remarks took me back to my suspicion about the documents produced by Ferdinand Baumhauer as well as the policemen interviewing Konstanzer Hans. These documents had been produced under duress and by people with every interest of hiding their true identity, and now I learned that the same process was still going on.

Miche also confirmed something I had long suspected, that Rotwelsch had functioned as a kind of lingua franca of the underground. He reported that Rotwelsch terms were used for communication across different nomadic groups that did not have another language in common. He also told me that the groups he was in contact with still used *zinken*, though guardedly. He mentioned that he had reported a sighting of some *zinken* to the chief of a group of nomads, who had promptly punished those who had used those *zinken* irresponsibly, attracting unwanted attention.

I felt extremely grateful that Miche had won the trust of a group of nomads, one of the few outsiders to do so, and that he in turn trusted me, giving me a window onto a world I thought had disappeared. The cat-and-mouse game with the police; the deeply rooted secrecy; the *zinken*; the association and dissociation with Sinti and Roma; the difficulties of maintaining a nomadic lifestyle in the face of opposition from the state—all these struggles were strikingly similar to what I had found in the long history of Rotwelsch.

As I was contemplating my good fortune, I received another email from him: he had set up a meeting with the Chief (as he called him). Miche would be told of the time and place of the meeting only an hour beforehand, and the meeting would take place in a truck. He described to me how difficult it was to speak to members of this group. "They respond in their own way. When they finish their meal, they can't stay still for five minutes." He would be driving around with the Chief on back roads for dozens, perhaps even hundreds, of miles. If I wanted, he would convey some questions on my behalf. With fingers shaking from excitement, I fired off a few questions and waited.

The next day, I received a series of long answers that were both surprising and deeply moving. For one thing, the Chief launched into a harangue against those Yenish speakers who had allowed themselves to be settled permanently. Speaking in French, he held them responsible for the demise of Yenish and the nomadic life that sustained it. The Chief went on to describe the misery of settled life more generally. Still addressing Miche, he said:

> If, in your town, you look at the ceiling, you don't see it for what it is. What I say is this, that you citizens love false ceilings and appearances. You don't even recognize the true ceilings, which you prefer to misrecognize. You don't know the superb landscapes and backdrops that you have where you live. But I know them and I can describe to you what you have in your own homes.

I puzzled over these sentences, which seemed to move abruptly between indoors and outdoors, ceilings and landscapes. Miche and the Chief had crossed into the Bernese countryside, which is one of the most beautiful in the world, the subject of the most cliched postcards of Swiss mountain bliss and even scenes from Bollywood films. I think this was what the Yenish Chief was driving at: we settled people can't really see this scenery because all we do is make postcards of it. For the same reason, sedentary life was a false life, and those who adopted it were incapable of recognizing the distinction between true and false. This was also why the Chief was so harsh about sedentary Yenish speakers: they had opted for a false life even though they should know better.

I had asked specifically about language, how this group of Yenish speakers understood their language and its different sources. The Chief answered:

> You have to understand that we vagrants [he used the word *voyageurs*, or travelers] have always recycled things. For centuries, we have recycled bones to make soap. Then we recycled metals. Then we recycled other materials. We love recycling things because this allows us to maintain our traditions. This is our mode of life.

All these years I had been looking for a term to characterize Rotwelsch, and here it was: recycling. This was the right word for a lifestyle that relied on reusing materials produced by the sedentary world, materials taken from cities or found along the road. Recycling, rather than making things from scratch, was the tradition of vagrants, and only by recycling could that tradition be preserved.

Recycling was particularly important for language. Rotwelsch and its younger variants consisted exclusively of recycled words, words taken from the languages produced by the world around them, from German, Czech, and various Romance languages as well as from other nomadic languages such as Yiddish and Romani. These recycled words had been given new meanings in the secretive world of the underground, forming a tradition going back hundreds of years. True, other languages are recycled as well, but we rarely remember this fact about them. We think we're speaking proper languages, languages with armies and navies, languages into which the Bible and other works of world literature have been translated, when in fact we're making ourselves understood, badly enough, with words preowned by others. Even Ludwig Zamenhof didn't invent a new language from scratch, but used a dozen existing languages when he created Esperanto. But among all these languages, Rotwelsch and Yenish were recycled most fully and most self-consciously, languages that wore recycling proudly on their sleeves.

I had also asked about the distinction between Yenish and Rotwelsch, because Miche had mentioned the existence of a good number of Rotwelsch words in Yenish, something I had found as well. He had said that Yenish speakers were sometimes hesitant to admit this, partly because of their ingrained secrecy but also because of the negative association of Rotwelsch with crime, an association Yenish speakers understandably wanted to avoid.

While Miche and I were happy to compare notes on the relation between Yenish and Rotwelsch, the Chief was having none of it: "I don't understand," he said to me, via Miche,

why sedentary people love dissecting words so much. I am

Yenish, and if I say anything else, I would no longer be
Yenish. I don't understand Rotwelsch and Yiddish words, I
know them only if they have become Yenish. Our language
is rich. I don't see why I should make distinctions within
Yenish; to cut something into different parts, that's the vice
of the city.

I had to plead guilty to this charge. I love making distinctions,
analyzing words, cutting them up into pieces and looking at
them under a magnifying glass. Dissecting words is what scholars do, and scholars are the product of cities, the ultimate outgrowth of sedentary life. It is not, of course, what speakers of
a language normally do; they just speak it. The Chief's remark
put me in my place, the place of a scholar who sought to understand nomadic life by reading a dictionary.

The tendency of settled people to make distinctions made
the Chief laugh. He laughed at me, the foolish dissector of language, the city dweller, the asker of inopportune questions via
an intermediary with whom the Chief was driving around in a
truck in the Bernese countryside. There was only one reaction
to so much ignorance, a reaction that wasn't even a word anymore but simply a sound: laughter.

I didn't actually hear this laughter, of course, because it was
conveyed to me by my correspondent, in writing, as an aside,
which reminded me of the stage directions Ferdinand Baumhauer had added to his Rotwelsch scenes. But even though I
didn't hear this laughter, I think I understood it. This laughter
acknowledged the unbridgeable gulf between nomadic life and
the attempts on the part of sedentary, distinction-making city
dwellers such as myself to understand it. It was laughter that
seemed to be directed equally at Martin Luther, generations of

policemen, welfare workers, social reform programs, housing projects, and scholars pestering Yenish and Rotwelsch speakers with questions about the language; it was laughter that was aimed at my grandfather and his campaign against Rotwelsch, but also at my uncle and his attempt to revive it through literature; and of course this laughter was above all directed at myself.

If you had asked me earlier about my position with respect to this language, I would have replied that I wrote as an ally, mitigating as best as I could the centuries of prosecution inflicted on these speakers by settled society. But what did it really mean, to write as an ally? It was a self-serving story I had concocted to convince myself that I was doing some sort of reparative work. There had been only one appropriate response to so much folly: to laugh in my face.

But there was something else I detected in the Chief's laughter: a delight in his language. The laughter spoke to me about the wit and lightness of Rotwelsch, a wit and lightness not lessened by the harsh realities of life on the road but born from them. These speakers had preserved a tradition despite centuries of prosecution and were continuing it against all opposition. You will never know this language, the laughter was saying, because you live in another world, a false world. Only I know just how false this world is, and my whole way of life, my entire language, is one big laughter with which we, the *kochemer*, the ones in the know, make fun of you. We know you, but you will never know us.

When the Chief was done laughing, he drove off into the mountains.

Acknowledgments

Writing about my own family has been hard, hard on me and hard on them, which is why I want to begin by thanking all family members for their forbearance. The story I tell about my grandfather and how his life choices have shaped subsequent generations is based on my own memories, thoughts, and emotions, as well as my own research, and I understand that others have stories of their own.

Over the many years of its gestation, the book received support from a number of individuals and institutions. I found the courage to tackle this topic only when Amanda Claybaugh thought I was on the right track and to stop when she declared that I was done. Friends and colleagues were exceptionally generous in reading and commenting on the evolving manuscript, including Jesse Ball, David Damrosch, Catherine Lacey, Laura Strausfeld, and Saul Zaritt. I received additional advice from Ava Chin, Sam Haselby, Maya Jasanoff, and David Levine, as well as from Ross Perlin, who makes an appearance in the book.

I am particularly grateful to my steadfast agent, Jill Kneerim, who accompanied this project from its inception, as well as to Alane Mason, my editor at W. W. Norton, who was willing to take her chances with this book and who contributed significantly to shaping it. Mo Crist at Norton patiently guided me through the production process, and Trent Duffy did a wonderful job copy-editing the manuscript. I was delighted to work again with Bella Lacey, at Granta, who ruthlessly decluttered my prose, among many other contributions.

I was fortunate to spend a year at the Cullman Center of the New York Public Library, in the delightful company of Joan Acocella, Sarah Bridger, Ava Chin, Hugh Eakin, Blake Gopnik, Georgi Gospodinov, Nellie Hermann, Frances Jetter, Lynn Melnik, Melinda Moustakis, Lorrie Moore, Eyal Press, Magda Teter, and Barbara Weinstein, and in the care of Salvatore Scibona, Lauren Goldenberg, and Paul Delaverdac, all of whom created the atmosphere in which this book could come into being.

The book was completed at another wonderful institution, the American Academy in Berlin, where Jennifer Allen, Emily Apter, Jesse Ball, Fred M. Donner, Jared Farmer, Anne Finger, George Framton, Peter Holquist, Catherine Lacey, Wang Lu, Terry McCarthy, Ronald Radano, Lucy Raven, Mark Schwartz, Prerna Singh, and Tony Vidler were frequent and helpful interlocutors.

During this time, the book also received generous support from the Guggenheim Foundation and from the Dean's Fund for Promising Scholarship at Harvard University.

Many other friends and colleagues helped in all kinds of ways, including the 2019 class of the Mellon School of Theater and Performance Research, a summer school focused on migration, and the Harvard colleagues who participated in the Poggioli Seminar. I am also grateful to Sarah Cole, Rebecca Walkowitz, Elin Diamond, and Andrew Goldstone for their feedback at the Modernism Colloquium at Columbia University, to W. J. van Bekkum and Jesse Amselvoort for conversations at Groningen University, to R. Jay Magill and Anthony Andrews at the American Academy, as well as to Leonard Barkan, Debra Caplan, Jeremy Dauber, Leslie Dunton-Downer, Michael Eskin, Sander L. Gilman, Ariane Harrison, Seth Harrison, Daniel Heller-Roazen, Noah Herringman, Sharon Marcus, Luke Menand, Tore Rem, Bruce Robbins, Marc Shell, Alison Simmons, Michael Steinberg, Kathrin Stengel, David Stern, and Jean Strouse.

This is a book very much about archives and libraries, and the archival research necessary for this book was supported by Prof. Dr. Fleischmann, director of the Staatsarchiv Nuremberg, Dr. Susanne Millet at the Bayerisches Hauptstaatsarchiv, Constanze Mann at the Stadtarchiv Jena, Dr. Andreas Erb at the Landesarchiv Sachsen-Anhalt, Andreas Grunwald at the Bundesarchiv, Manfred Krey at the KZ-Gedänkstätte Schwäbisch Hall-Hessental, and Gebhard Füßler at the Landesarchiv Baden-Württemberg. I also want to thank Yolande Korb, librarian at the American Academy, Odile Harter, at Harvard's Widener Library, and the wonderful staff at the New York Public Library.

I was delighted that many people wrote to me with information about Rotwelsch after hearing that I was working on this language, including Heiner Holtbrügge and Michael Trzybinski. Among those correspondents, I would like to single out François Miche, whose thoughts and experiences with Yenish peoples ended up providing me with a final chapter.

I want to conclude by returning to Amanda Claybaugh, whose love sustained me during the many hours of writing of this book.

Notes

INTRODUCTION: LANGUAGE GAMES

1 Hans Gross, *Die Gaunerzinken der Freistädter Handschrift* (Leipzig, 1899), pl. 88.

2 Ibid., pl. 11; Hans Gross, *Handbuch für Untersuchungsrichter als System der Kriminalistik*, 5th ed. (Munich: J. Schweitzer Verlag, 1908), 356.

3 The idiom derives from the Yiddish idiom *Zores- und Jokreszeit* (time of need and price increases) and was assimilated to the similar-sounding German expression *Sauregurkenzeit* (cucumber time).

CHAPTER 1: CAMOUFLAGE NAMES

1 Karl Puchner, *Patronizienforschung und Eigenkirchenwesen, mit besonderer Berücksichtigung des Bistums Eichstätt* (Kallmünz: Buchdruckerei Michael Laßleben, 1932).

2 Karl Puchner, "Familiennamen als Rassenmerkmal," *Schriften des Bayerischen Landesvereins für Familienkunde* 4 (1934): 1–16.

3 Ibid., 14.

4 Ibid., 6.

5 Ibid., 13.

6 *Richtlinien über die Führung der Vornamen: Rundlerlaß des Reichsminister des Inneren* vom 18. August 1938 (I d 42 X/38-5501b), published in *Ministerialblatt des Reichs- und Preußischen Ministeriums des Inneren*, no. 35 (August 1938).

7 See Cornelia Essner, *Die Nürnberger Gesetze oder Die Verwaltung des Rassenwahns, 1933–1945* (Paderborn: Schöningh Verlag, 2002), 246ff.

8 See Uwe Dietrich Adam, *Judenpolitik im Dritten Reich* (Düsseldorf: Droste Verlag, 1988), 61ff. Also see Deborah Hertz, "The Genealogy Bureaucracy in the Third Reich," *Jewish History* 11, no. 2 (Fall

1997): 53–78, and Gudrun Exner and Peter Schimany, "Amtliche Statistik und Judenverfolgung," in *Geschichte und Gesellschaft* 32, no. 1 (January–March 2006): 93–118.

9 Sybil Milton, "Registering Civilians and Aliens in the Second World War," *Jewish History* 11, no. 2 (Fall 1997): 84.

CHAPTER 2: THE BOOK OF VAGRANTS

1 Account based on Veit-Jakobus Dieterich, *Martin Luther: Sein Leben und seine Zeit* (Stuttgart: Deutsche Verlagsgesellschaft, 2017), among others.

2 Martin Puchner, *The Written World: The Power of Stories to Change People, History, and Civilization* (New York: Random House, 2017), 145ff.

3 Martin Luther, *Von der falschen Bettler büberey / Mit einer Vorrede Martini Luther. Und hinden an ein Rotwelsch Vocabularius / darauß man die wörter / so in dysem büchlein gebrauch / verstehen kann* (Wittenberg, 1528).

4 Ibid., 1.

5 Martin Luther, *Von den Juden und iren Lügen* (Wittenberg: Hans Lufft, 1543).

6 For the long history of Christian anti-Judaism, see David Nirenberg, *Anti-Judaism: The Western Tradition* (New York: Norton, 2013).

7 Henry Kamen, "The Economic and Social Consequences of the Thirty Years' War," *Past and Present*, no. 39 (April 1968): 44–61.

CHAPTER 4: THE ROTWELSCH INHERITANCE

1 See Casten Küther, *Räuber und Gauner in Deutschland: Das organisierte Bandenwesen im 18 und frühen 19 Jahrhundert* (Göttingen: Vandenhoeck und Ruprecht, 1976), 34ff.

2 Ibid., 76.

3 Hans Gross, *Handbuch für Untersuchungsrichter als System der Kriminalistik*, 5th ed. (Munich: J. Schweitzer Verlag, 1908), 356.

4 Account based on Wilhelm Friedrich Wüst, *Der Konstanzer Hans: Merkwürdige Geschichte eines schwäbischen Gauners* (Reutlingen: Fleischhauer und Spohn, 1852), and Johann Ulrich Schöll, *Konstanzer Hanß: Eine schwäbische Jauners-Geschichte aus zuverlässigen Quellen geschöpft und pragmatisch bearbeitet* (Stuttgart: Erhard und Löflund, 1791).

5 Wüst, *Der Konstanzer Hans*, 100.

6 Ibid., 1.

7 Küther, *Räuber und Gauner in Deutschland*, 84.

8 Alexander Beider, *Origins of Yiddish Dialects* (Oxford: Oxford University Press, 2015), 1ff.

9 Max Weinreich, *Geshikhte Fun der Yidisher Shprak* (New York: Yidisher Visnshaftlekher Institut, 1973).

10 Frederick Speidel Youkstetter, "Friedrich Christian Benedict Ave-Lallemant, His Life and His Fiction" (Ph.D. diss., University of Chicago, December 1949). Also see Daniel Heller-Roazen, *Dark Tongues: The Art of Rogues and Riddlers* (Cambridge, Mass.: MIT Press, 2013), 36ff.

11 Friedrich Christian Benedict Avé-Lallemant, *Das Deutsche Gaunerthum* (Leipzig: Brockhaus, 1858).

12 Based on his daughter's notes, which were included in the 1914 edition of his *Das Deutsche Gaunerthum*, edited by Max Bauer (Munich: G. Müller, 1914), vi.

13 Martin Puchner, *The Written World: The Power of Stories to Change People, History, and Civilization* (New York: Random House, 2017), 271.

14 Adolf Hitler, *Mein Kampf* (Munich: Zentralverlag der NSDAP, 1943), 135.

15 Ibid., 70.

16 Ibid., 68.

17 Ibid., 342; Sander L. Gilman, *Jewish Self-Hatred: Anti-Semitism and the Hidden Language of the Jews* (Baltimore: The Johns Hopkins University Press, 1985).

18 Gilman, *Jewish Self-Hatred*, 71ff.

19 Hitler, *Mein Kampf*, 337.

20 Reinhold Hanisch, "I Was Hitler's Buddy," *The New Republic*, April 5, 1939.

21 Brigitte Hamann, *Hitler's Vienna: A Portrait of the Tyrant as a Young Man* (Oxford: Oxford University Press, 1999).

22 Hanisch, "I Was Hitler's Buddy."

CHAPTER 5: THE KING OF THE TRAMPS

1 The journal, *Aspekte/Impulse: Zeitschrift für Literatur und Grafik*, was published by Günter und Herbert Puchner Verlag, starting in November 1963 and continuing through 1969.

2 Klaus Trappmann, ed., *Landstrasse, Kunden, Vagabunden: Gregor Gogs Liga der Heimatlosen* (Berlin: Gerhardt Verlag, 1980), 11ff.

3 Ibid., 83.

4 Ibid., 48.
5 Ibid., 131.
6 Ibid., 223.
7 Ibid., 128.
8 *Der Vagabund*, dir. Fritz Weiß, 1930; silent, with Dutch intertitles, 35mm; Bundesarchiv-Filmarchiv, Berlin, #BSP-24428ß5.
9 Trappmann, *Landstrasse*, 263.
10 Ibid.
11 Ibid., 97.
12 Ibid., 143.
13 Ibid., 114.
14 Siegmund A. Wolf, *Wörterbuch des Rotwelschen: Deutsche Gaunersprache* (Mannheim: Bibliographisches Institut, 1956), 160. Writing in Gog's journal, one vagrant also related the term to *kochemer*, to know: see Trappman, *Landstrasse*, 58. The term might also be related to the Yiddish *kundes*, for prankster.
15 Trappmann, *Landstrasse*, 59.
16 Ibid., 58.
17 Ibid., 30.
18 Ibid., 30ff.
19 Ibid., 227.
20 Ibid., 32.
21 "Acta," Jena Police Commission, 1843, Jena State Archives, B files, abt. IX, no. 6a, vols. 1 and 2. Part of this source was published in Karl Spangenberg, *Baumhauers Stromergespräche in Rotwelsch: Mit soziologischen und sprachlichen Erläuterungen* (Halle: Max Niemeyer Verlag, 1970).
22 Hans Gross, *Die Gaunerzinken der Freistädter Handschrift* (Leipzig, 1899), pl. 27, 34, 15, and 14.

CHAPTER 6: THE FARMER AND THE JUDGE

1 Hannsjoachim W. Koch, *Volksgerichtshof: Politische Justiz im 3 Reich* (Munich: Universitas Verlag, 1988).
2 Alan E. Steinweis and Robert D. Rachlin, eds., *The Law in Nazi Germany: Ideology, Opportunism, and the Perversion of Justice* (New York: Berghahn, 2013).
3 Astrid Ley and Günter Morsch, *Medizin und Verbrechen: Das Krankenrevier des KZ Sachsenhausen, 1936–1945* (Berlin: Metropol, 2007).

4 Gerhard Finn, *Sachsenhausen, 1936–1950: Geschichte Eines Lagers* (Bonn: Urheber, 1985).

5 Primo Levi, *The Drowned and the Saved*, trans. Michael F. Moore, *The Complete Works of Primo Levi*, ed. Ann Goldstein (New York: Liveright/Norton, 2016), 3:2478.

6 Ibid., 3:2476.

7 Ibid., 3:2460.

8 Primo Levi, *If This Is a Man*, trans. Stuart Moore, in Goldstein, *The Complete Works of Primo Levi*, 1:34.

9 Günter Morsch, ed., *Sachsenhausen-Liederbuch*, facsimile ed. (Berlin: Edition Heinrich, 1995).

10 Siegmund A. Wolf, *Wörterbuch des Rotwelschen: Deutsche Gaunersprache* (Mannheim: Bibliographisches Institut, 1956), 220.

11 Oberlandesgerichtspräsident Dr. Küstner to Minister of Justice, OJs 12-44, Stuttgart, June 3, 1944, Bundesarchivbestand Nationalsozialistische Justiz (R 3018) Strafprozessakten unter der Signatur R 3018 (alt NJ)/2739, p. 50.

12 Roland Freisler, Bs 96-44, 5 J 1230-44, *"er ist nämlich, wie man ihm ansieht, sehr beschränkt."* Bundesarchivbestand Nationalsozialistische Justiz, Signatur R 3018 (alt NJ)/2739.

13 Document provided by Landesarchiv Sachsen-Anhalt, Abteilung Dessau, Z 295 Zuchthaus Coswig, document 1228 (old number 897/440), pp. 1–3 (January 12, 1945).

14 Edda Ahrberg, Alexander Fuhrmann, and Jutta Preiß, *Das Zuchthaus Coswig (Anhalt)* (Magdeburg: Landesbeauftragter für die Unterlagen des Staatssicherheitsdienstes, 2007), 31.

15 Ibid., 49.

16 Bessel van der Kolk, *The Body Keeps the Score: Brain, Mind, and Body in the Healing of Trauma* (New York: Penguin, 2014), 193.

CHAPTER 7: AN ATTIC IN PRAGUE

1 Nelly Sachs, *Fahrt ins Staublose* (Frankfurt am Main: Suhrkamp, 1988).

2 Evelyn Tornton Beck, *Kafka and the Yiddish Theater* (Madison: University of Wisconsin Press, 1971). See also my "Kafka's Antitheatrical Gestures," *The Germanic Review* 78, no. 3 (issue titled "Kafka and the Theater," edited by Martin Puchner) (Summer 2003): 177–93.

3 Debra Caplan, *Yiddish Empire: The Vilna Troupe, Jewish Theater, and the Art of Itinerancy* (Ann Arbor: University of Michigan Press, 2018).

4 Franz Kafka, "Rede über die jiddische Sprache," in *Hochzeitsvorbereitungen auf dem Lande und andere Prosa aus dem Nachlaß*, ed. Max Brod (Frankfurt am Main: Fischer, 1983), 306.

5 Rudolf Fröhlich, *Die gefährlichen Klassen Wiens* (Wein: Benedikt's Buchhandlung, 1851).

6 Karl Treimer, "Das tschechische Rotwelsch," in *Slavica: Beiträge zum Studium der Sprache, Literatur, Kultur, Volks- und Altertumskunde der Slaven*, vol. 12, eds. Karl H. Meyer and M. Murko (Heidelberg: Carl Winters Universitätsbuchhandlung, 1937), 6.

7 Ibid., 12.

8 Arguments that Kafka wrote in a nonstandard German, presented by Gilles Deleuze and Félix Guattari in *Kafka: For a Minor Literature*, translated by Dana Polan (Minneapolis: University of Minnesota Press, 1986), have proven to be wrong. Also see David Suchoff, *Kafka's Jewish Languages: The Hidden Openness of Tradition* (Philadelphia: University of Pennsylvania Press, 2012).

9 Hartmut Binder, *Gustav Meyrink: Ein Leben im Bann der Magie* (Prague: Vitalis, 2009), 545.

10 Resene Gibronte Runeclus Hanedi, *Steganologia and Steganographia NOVA* (Nuremberg: Simon Halbmayer, 1627), 14ff. Also see Friedrich Kluge, *Rotwelsch: Quellen und Wortschatz der Gaunersprache und der verwandten Geheimsprachen* (Straßburg: Karl J. Trübner, 1901), 132ff.

CHAPTER 8: WHEN JESUS SPOKE ROTWELSCH

1 Günter Puchner, *Kundenschall: Das Gekasper der Kirschenpflücker im Winter* (Munich: Heimeran, 1974), 178.

2 Max Weinreich, "YIVO and the Problems of Our Time," *YIVO Bleter* 23, no. 3 (January–June 1944).

3 Ibid., 274–77.

4 Puchner, *Kundenschall*, 114.

5 The novel was translated by Peter Perring Thoms, *Chinese Courtship: In Verse; To Which Is Added, an Appendix, Treating of the Revenue of China* (London: Parbury, Allen, and Kingsbury, 1824).

6 Johann Peter Eckermann, *Gespräche mit Goethe in den letzten Jahren seines Lebens*, 2 vols. (Leipzig: Brockhaus, 1837), 1:322.

7 Ibid., 1:325.

8 David Suchoff, *Kafka's Jewish Languages: The Hidden Openness of Tradition* (Philadelphia: University of Pennsylvania Press, 2012), 48.

9 Melekh Ravitsh and Borekh Rivkin, "Reflections on World Litera-

ture," in *World Literature in Theory*, ed. David Damrosch (Chichester, Eng.: Blackwell/Wiley, 2013): 71–84.

10 Hoffmann von Fallersleben, *Weimarisches Jahrbuch*, vol. 4 (Hannover: Carl Rümpler, 1856), 330.

11 Günter Puchner to Noack-Hübner-Verlag, November 28, 1981.

12 Günter Puchner, *Ein Arm voll Schmonzes* (Frankfurt am Main: Edition Fischer, 1983).

CHAPTER 9: IGPAY ATINLAY FOR ADULTS

1 Marjorie Boulton, *Zamenhof, Creator of Esperanto* (London: Routledge, 1960). Also see Esther Schor, *Bridge of Words: Esperanto and the Dream of a Universal Language* (New York: Metropolian Books/Henry Holt, 2016).

2 Franz Kafka, "Fragments," in *Hochzeitsvorbereitungen auf dem Lande und andere Prosa aus dem Nachlaß*, ed. Max Brod (Frankfurt am Main: Fischer, 1983), 280.

3 Ulrich Lins, *Die gefährliche Sprache: Die Verfolgung der Esperantisten unter Hitler und Stalin* (Gerlingen: Bleicher Verlag, 1988), 47.

4 Adolf Hitler, *Mein Kampf* (Munich: Zentralverlag der NSDAP, 1943), 337.

5 Rudolf Carnap, "The Elimination of Metaphysics Through Logical Analysis of Language," trans. Arthur Pap, in *Logical Positivism*, ed. A. J. Ayer (Glencoe, Ill.: Free Press, 1959), 60–81.

6 Roberto Garvía, *Esperanto and Its Rivals: The Struggle for an International Language* (Philadelphia: University of Pennsylvania Press, 2015), 88.

7 G. W. Leibniz, *Neue Abhandlung über den menschlichen Verstand* (Hamburg: Felix Meiner Verlag, 1971), 302.

CHAPTER 10: THE STORY OF AN ARCHIVIST

1 Karl Puchner, personnel file, Bayerisches Hauptstaatsarchiv, Generaldirektion der Staatlichen Archive (hereinafter GDion Archive), file 3063; additional documents pertaining to Karl Puchner are held under Überlieferung des Reichsstatthalters in Bayern, file 7103.

2 Karl Puchner, personnel file, GDion Archive, file 3063, p. 57.

3 Matthias Berg, *Karl Alexander von Müller: Historiker für den Nationalsozialismus* (Göttingen: Vandenhoeck und Ruprecht, 2014).

4 Karl Puchner, "Oath of Office," October 10, 1934, personnel file, GDion Archive, file 3063.

5 Karl Puchner, "Professional Performance Review," March 16, 1938, in ibid.

6 Karl Puchner, Spruchkammerakte, SpkA K 1358, declaration by Karl Puchner, June 23, 1946, in ibid.

7 Dr. Riedner to Karl Puchner April 21, 1934, in ibid.

CHAPTER 11: JUDGMENT AT HIKELS-MOKUM

1 Victor Klemperer, *I Will Bear Witness: A Diary of the Nazi Years*, translated by Martin Chalmers (New York: Random House, 1998).

2 Victor Klemperer, *The Language of the Third Reich*, translated by Martin Brady (London: Athlone Press, 2000).

3 Ancillary Personnel File I-120, Otto Puchner, and Nuremberg II Chamber of Appeals sig. P-177, Nuremberg State Archives.

4 Otto Puchner, "Die Ortsnamen im Bezirk Dinkelsbühl als Zeugen germanisch-deutscher Besiedlung" (Ph.D. diss. Ludwig Maximilan University of Munich, 1939).

CHAPTER 12: ERROR-SPANGLED BANNER

1 Jacob Weisberg, "W.'s Greatest Hits: The top 25 Bushisms of all time," *Slate*, January 12, 2009; https://slate.com/news-and-politics/2009/01/the-top-25-bushisms-of-all-time.html, accessed March 24, 2020.

2 Feridun Zaimoğlu, *Kanak Sprak* (Hamburg: Rotbuch Verlag, 1995).

3 Martin Puchner, "Guantanamo Bay," *London Review of Books* 26, no. 24 (December 16, 2004).

CHAPTER 14: ROTWELSCH IN AMERICA

1 Stan Richards and Associates, *Hobo Signs: A Lament for the Demise of the Most Communicative Symbolism of Them All* (New York: Barlenmir House, 1974).

2 Endangered Language Alliance, http://elalliance.org/why/, accessed November 24, 2018.

3 Kenneth Locke Hale, as quoted in "About Us" section of Endangered Languge Alliance website, https://elalliance.org/why/, accessed January 5, 2020.

4 Ehsan Yarshater, "The Hybrid Language of the Jewish Communities of Persia," *Journal of the American Oriental Society* 97, no. 1 (January–March 1977): 1–7.

5 Karl Treimer, "Das tschechische Rotwelsch," in *Slavica: Beiträge zum*

Studium der Sprache, Literatur, Kultur, Volks- und Altertumskunde der Slaven, vol. 12, eds. Karl H. Meyer and M. Murko (Heidelberg: Carl Winters Universitätbuchshandlung, 1937), 14.

6 Gillian Trett, "Have We Learnt the Lessons of the Financial Crisis?," *Financial Times*, August 31, 2018; https://www.ft.com/content /a9b25e40-ac37-11e8-89a1-e5de165fa619, accessed November 18, 2019. Investigators going through Lehman Brothers emails identified particular phrases that indicated incriminating correspondence: see Jacob Goldstein, "23 Things Not to Write in an E-mail," NPR, June 14, 2010; https://www.npr.org/sections/money/2010/06/14/127829646/23 -things-not-to-say-in-an-email, accessed November 16, 2019.

7 Ludwig Wittgenstein, *Philosophical Investigations*, trans. G. E. M. Anscombe (Oxford: Blackwell, 1953).

8 Claims that the two had a profound impact on each other, however, are far-fetched. An argument for such an influence was made in Kimberley Cornish, *The Jew of Linz: Hitler, Wittgenstein and the Meeting Between Them That Changed the Course of History* (New York: Century Books, 1998).

CHAPTER 15: THE LAUGHTER OF A YENISH CHIEF

1 Rudolf Jaworski, "'Böhmischer Zirkel'—Anmerkungen zur Karriere einer Bildchiffre aus der Wiener Gaunersprache," *Österreichische Zeitschrift für Volkskunde* LXIX/118 (2015), volume 1+2, 41–50.

2 Roland Girtler, *Rotwelsch: Die Alte Sprache der Gauner, Dirnen und Vagabunden* (Vienna: Bohlau, 1998), 141.

Illustration Credits

96 Line drawing of hobo *zinken* with translation. Source: Gross, Gauner-zinken, plate 14.

130 Photograph of Alt-Neu Synagogue of Prague. Taken by the author.

145 Reproduction of book cover, *Ein Arm voll Schmonzes*, by Günther Puchner (Frankfurt am Main: R. G. Fischer 1983). Copyright: R. G. Fischer Verlag.

162 Statue in front of Bavarian State Archive, Munich. Taken by the author.

187 Photograph of Nuremberg War Crimes Trial. National Archives and Records Administration.

223 Line drawings of American hobo signs. Author rendering.

Index